Building Garden Furniture

More Than 30 Beautiful Outdoor Projects

Ray Martin &
Lee Rankin

A Sterling/Lark Book
Sterling Publishing Co., Inc.   New York

Editor: Chris Rich
Art Director: Chris Colando
Production: Elaine Thompson, Chris Colando, Charlie Covington
Photography: Evan Bracken
Illustrations: Don Osby

Library of Congress Cataloging-in-Publication Data

Martin, Ray, 1943–
   Building garden furniture : more than 30 beautiful outdoor projects / Ray Martin
 and Lee Rankin.
      p.   cm.
   "A Sterling/Lark book."
   Includes index.
   ISBN 0-8069-8374-4
   1. Outdoor furniture.   I. Rankin, Lee, 1945–   .   II. Title.
 TT197.5.09M37   1993
 684.1'8--dc20

                                                                    92-37217
                                                                    CIP

10   9

A Sterling/Lark Book

First paperback edition published in 1994 by
Sterling Publishing Company, Inc.
387 Park Avenue South, New York, N.Y. 10016

Produced by Altamont Press, Inc.
50 College Street, Asheville, NC 28801

© 1993 by Altamont Press

Distributed in Canada by Sterling Publishing
   % Canadian Manda Group, P.O. Box 920, Station U
   Toronto, Ontario, Canada M8Z 5P9
Distributed in Great Britain and Europe by Cassell PLC
   Villiers House, 41/47 Strand, London WC2N 5JE, England
Distributed in Australia by Capricorn Link Ltd.
   P.O. Box 665, Lane Cove, NSW 2066

Every effort has been made to ensure that all the information in this book is
accurate. However, due to differing conditions, tools, and individual skills,
the publisher cannot be responsible for any injuries, losses, and other
damages which may result from the use of the information in this book.

Sterling ISBN 0-8069-8374-4 Trade
                0-8069-8375-2 Paper

CONTENTS

INTRODUCTION

Gardens are as different as their owners, but whatever yours looks like—whether it's formal or wild, small or large, shaded or bathed in sunlight—if you're rarely in it, you probably aren't enjoying it much. How much time do you spend in your yard these days? As much time as it takes to trudge between the car and your back door? If you think of your garden as a pathway to your house or a view from a window, chances are what's missing in your life is neither time itself, nor the perfect green setting, but outdoor furniture that will invite you to stay awhile.

Lingering in the fresh air is never quite as appealing when there's nowhere to stretch out, nowhere to rest a fragrant cup of hot coffee or glass of iced tea, nowhere to relax. But a bench that beckons, a table designed for outdoor dining, a distinctive chair, recliner, or hammock—even a single swing, swaying under a favorite tree—can transform your unused yard into an area just as attractive and almost as frequently occupied as any room in the house.

You can purchase ready-made outdoor furniture, of course. Bargain-store picnic tables aren't hard to find, but why settle for less than the best when you can build furniture that's a cut above the common—furniture designed to be good-looking and long-lasting? Worried about your woodworking skills? Don't be. You don't have to be a master with wood to create the projects in this book. Though they weren't designed for beginners, the average woodworker should be able to complete any of them with confidence.

We've simplified all projects by presenting them with clear, step-by-step instructions and detailed illustrations. We've also included special lists of tools, materials, hardware, and supplies—lists that will help you to minimize costs and save time. And if you haven't done much woodworking recently, the first two chapters will bring your fading skills back to life.

As you browse through the projects, you'll notice that many of them make use of similar design elements. Once you've built the back for the Chippendale chair, for instance, making one for the Chippendale bench should be a breeze because the two are almost exactly the same. Those shared stylistic elements also make it possible to group individual pieces in handsome combinations. Consider the photographs of lush garden settings too. These offer new perspectives—new ways to visualize your yard and the furniture you'll be displaying in it.

In one weekend, you can gift yourself—or a deserving friend—with more than an eye-catching, new piece of furniture. Just a few hours in your workshop will also yield an entirely new garden—one you can't wait to occupy. Once your finished project has found its place (under a shade tree, by a path, next to an herb bed or pond), you'll find that your neglected garden becomes a much-loved part of your life and home.

CHAPTER ONE
BEFORE YOU BEGIN

The urge to dash off and purchase lumber may have struck already, but before you give in, invest a little time in preparation. Your project is much more likely to satisfy you if you've chosen it wisely and if you've taken some steps to ensure that your workshop is organized and safe before you start.

PLANNING

Classic garden furniture looks well almost anywhere—but why not make sure that the pieces you choose are the ones best suited to your garden—and to your personal tastes? You'll have a lot of fun building the hammock stand, for instance, but if your property is situated on the slope of a steep, rocky hill, you might want to put this project last on your personal wish-list and first on the list of gifts you can build for a friend who owns level land. Whether you plan to keep and enjoy what you make or endow a friend's back yard, planning is the crucial first step.

You don't need a landscape architect to tell you which pieces of furniture are best suited to your garden's design. Just grab a notebook, and step outdoors. Study your garden, and record what you see. Ask yourself questions, and write down your answers. Is the entire area in full sunlight all day long? Which areas are always shaded? Where is the ground most level? Will moisture be a persistent problem in some areas, but not in others? What about the look and feel of your garden? Which areas seem most appealing to you—and why? Try to picture a given piece of furniture in your favorite spot. Is it large enough? Does it block a view of another attractive spot? Should it be painted to complement the colors of your house, or would a colorless finish blend in better?

Once you've analyzed your garden, purchase some graph paper, and make a scale drawing of your lot. To get some sense of how the garden will look once furniture is added, draw and then cut a miniature planter, bench, or cart from scrap paper, and move these models around on the sketched plan until each item has found its ideal spot.

Familiarity with your garden will help you to choose furniture that's right for it, but it's equally important to get in touch with your own personal tastes. Imagine a few pleasant garden scenarios: sitting in the shade and sipping an iced drink on a midsummer afternoon, serving a formal dinner for four on a lantern-lit dining table, massaging more lotion into your tan as you stretch out on a chaise, reading while you laze in your hammock. Which scene appeals to you most? Start with the project that best fits the fantasy. Daydreams are just goals in disguise; if you nourish the ones that recur—and furnish them—they'll soon be realities.

THE WORKSHOP

Once you've selected a project, take a look at your workshop. You don't have to own an elaborate one to build the furniture in this book. But a designated work space can provide you with a built-in way to keep organized, safe, and attentive. Working while you're out on the back porch or in the yard is possible, but it isn't easy, and it isn't quite as much fun. Your working area should be dry, well-ventilated, well-lit, clean, and large enough to accommodate both you and your tools.

Consider your workshop's contents. Then, before you dash off to buy new equipment, refer to the list of suggested tools that accompanies each project, and read the sections in the next chapter which describe each tool and its use. You're likely to find that you won't need to make many special purchases.

Select a specific space for every tool you own, and make a practice of putting tools back when they're not in use. Label shelves and drawers (and the tools if necessary) so that you'll remember where everything belongs. Try hanging tools on pegboards, where they'll be visible, and using a marker to outline the shape of each one. A quick glance at the board will tell you if any tool is missing. Keep blades and bits sharp, and keep all tools free of dirt and rust.

SAFETY

Beginning woodworkers sometimes think that workshop safety is a matter of common sense. We disagree. Common sense tells us why the guard on a table saw exists and why we shouldn't stick our hands in front of moving blades. Yet guards still gather dust on workshop shelves, and emergency room staffs still make a decent living. Why? Because common sense bites the sawdust when it faces two favorite rationalizations: "Just this once," and "It won't happen to me."

Well, once is all it takes, and it can happen to you. Don't depend on your common sense. Know the dangers, and work on developing lifelong safety habits instead. Make sure, for instance, that you know what goggles are, and then set your vanity aside. Yes, you'll look like the Frog Prince or Princess of Woodworking when you wear them, but don't pick up a power tool unless those goggles are where they should be—decorating your face.

Making exceptions to safety rules is like trying to scroll with a circular saw—pointless. One exception can defeat every other effort you've made to protect your life and limbs. Be consistent. Practice doing things the right way. Before long, the right way will be second nature to you, and you won't have to depend on common sense.

The list that follows is brief and includes only general safety rules. For specific safety tips, always read the inserts that come with your tools.

Working when tired or distracted

Don't! Your body and mind need to be on the alert when you work with wood, so if you're exhausted or upset, take a nap or beat up a pillow. Your project can wait.

Fire and smoke

The one tool you shouldn't be without, but should never have to use, is a fire extinguisher. Don't smoke in your shop; sawdust, oils, and finishes can ignite. Avoid using power tools when there are flammable gases in the air. Check electrical cords for frays or cuts, and keep your shop as close to spotless as you can.

Clothing and jewelry

Loose clothing has a tendency to gravitate toward moving parts—parts like saw blades and drill bits. If you don't want your body to follow in the same direction, wear close-fitting clothes, and roll up your sleeves. Take your jewelry off—watches and wedding bands too.

Cleanliness

Place soiled rags in a covered, metal container, and empty it regularly. Bits of wood, tools, and trash on the floor are invitations to a bad fall; remove them as quickly as they appear. Tools and scraps on table saw surfaces can catch in blades and be thrown back at you.

Long hair

Tuck it up in a hat or net, or tie it back. Long hair loves to dance, but you won't love what happens when it tangos with a moving blade or bit.

Power tool safety

Saws with moving blades come with blade guards. When they don't appear in a book's photographs, assume that they've been removed only to show you parts or processes that can't be seen when they're where they should be. Keep the blade guard in place whenever you use the tool! And never stand in front of a blade; shift your body to one side of it.

Purchase double-insulated tools or ground them, and don't use power tools if your feet are anywhere near water. Before you adjust any of your tools, or change bits or blades, unplug the cord. Check the cords frequently too.

Ventilation

An open window won't do. If you're working indoors, install an exhaust fan, so that air and the nasty things in it circulate away from you. Even an ordinary fan will help if it pushes tainted air away from your working area. Wear a dust mask to keep airborne particles like sawdust out of your lungs. When you're working with volatile substances, wear a respirator that's designed to filter noxious fumes from the air—a dust mask won't do this job.

Noise

Extended exposure to loud noises can damage your hearing. You won't need ear plugs or protectors every moment, but make sure they're in (or on) when volume levels rise above normal.

Goggles

Wear them! Your loved ones will eventually forget how silly these protective devices make you look, but they're not likely to forget your losing an eye to a flying wood chip.

Children

There's nothing wrong with teaching children to work with wood, but the key word here is "teach." The good (and bad) habits we pick up as children tend to stick, so make sure that whenever a child is present in your workshop, you're there too—to teach good habits and to prevent mistakes.

CHAPTER TWO
BRUSHING UP

Most of you will be familiar—at least in passing— with the subjects handled in this chapter, so don't feel that you have to read it word-for-word. Treat it as a "refresher" course instead. Skim the sections that deal with matters you already know by heart, and delve into those that really interest you. If you have average woodworking skills, you could probably build any of our projects by simply reading the directions and materials lists included with them, but those of you whose skills are rusty will find that these sections offer pertinent, up-to-date information about the materials, tools, and techniques that you'll be using.

WOOD

Wood has its mysteries. Anyone who's felt a bit lost in the local lumberyard knows too well that there's more to a board than its width and length. And if you've ever had to choose from among wood species, you know how difficult it can be to evaluate, let alone identify, what you're looking at.

The garden furniture projects in this book don't require specialty woods. If you hate making choices, just use the recommended wood for each project. But if you enjoy decision-making, by all means choose another wood that pleases you. The information in this section will help you to make the best selections, whether you're purchasing lumber from a retail yard, a home improvement center, or a specialty-wood supplier. And if you'd like more information on lumber sizing, dimensions, and grades, just turn to pages 157–158, where we've included detailed information on these topics.

Wood Species

Wood's unique characteristics make it an ideal material for furniture construction. But what makes one type of wood different from another?

The major components of all wood are cellulose, which forms the framework of the wood cells or fibers; lignin, the cement layer between the cells; organic extractives, which impart the properties of color, rot resistance, density, and odor; and non-organic minerals such as calcium, magnesium, and potassium.

Variations in these elements make the difference between woods that are stiff rather than pliable, hard rather than soft, and light rather than dark. The components of each species are more or less constant, so a

wood's species serves as a yardstick for wood selection.

Trees (and the wood that comes from them) are divided into two categories: hardwoods and softwoods. But don't let the names fool you. A softwood such as Douglas fir or Southern longleaf (yellow) pine is actually harder than the hardwood popple Aspen.

As a general rule, softwood trees bear cones and typically have needle-like evergreen leaves, though a few species shed their needles in winter. Commercially available softwoods include pines, spruces, firs, and redwood. Hardwood trees have broad leaves and are deciduous, losing their leaves in the cold season.

For outdoor furniture construction, commercial softwoods are an excellent choice. They're reasonably priced and quite easy to work with. What's more, any retail lumberyard or home improvement center should stock a wide variety of dimensional lumber and plywood for framing, sheathing, or cabinetwork; you won't have any trouble finding softwoods for your garden furniture projects.

Commercial hardwoods—used for flooring, cabinetry, furniture, and pallet construction—are more expensive and not as easy to come by, though some retail outlets and mail-order houses supply them for home use. You're likely to have more access to hardwoods if you live in an area where such trees are harvested; independent suppliers such as sawmills and small manufacturers abound in these places. Hardwoods are also more difficult to work with than softwoods because they're ... well, harder, as well as denser. All these drawbacks are offset, however, by the fact that hardwoods cut more cleanly, are usually stronger, and have a more attractive appearance than most softwoods.

Weather Resistance and Rot

Every species of wood will eventually decay. Fungi-induced rot, brought on by the effects of moisture and exposure to the elements, takes its toll in due time. Of course, some species of wood are better at resisting this decay than others. If you plan to have a natural finish on your outdoor furniture, you'll need to either select a wood species that's decay-resistant or compromise with a wood product treated to withstand outdoor exposure. A third option is to finish the wood with a protective coating—a process that's addressed in detail on pages 12–14.

Naturally decay-resistant woods can be expensive and are sometimes difficult to obtain. Some long-lasting species, such as black locust, make wonderful fence posts, yet they're rarely used for furniture because they're hard, heavy, and difficult to work with. The more exotic species (mahogany, teak, or walnut) are certainly rot-resistant, but are also quite costly. Redwood, cedar, or even cypress all strike a happy medium; they're generally available and moderately priced. For standard yard lumber, Douglas fir makes an excellent choice because of its moderate cost and satisfactory decay resistance.

Treated woods are a good second choice because of their availability, excellent decay resistance, and moderate price. Any lumber outlet stocks a selection of pressure-treated woods which have undergone Fluor Chrome Arsenate Phenol (FCAP) treatment (sometimes referred to as Wolman or Osmose salt treatment) or a Chromated Copper Arsenate (CCA) process.

When shopping for treated wood, keep in mind that there are normally two degrees of treatment—a light-density retention level for above-ground use, and a heavier density level for below-ground applications. The more highly rated grades will naturally last longer when used outdoors.

Other treatments, such as pentachlorophenol and creosote solutions, have been used in the past to stave off the effects of weather and moisture on wood. In the United States, however, the Environmental Protection Agency has severely restricted the use of these toxic compounds, and products containing them are no longer available over the counter. The toxicity of even pressure-treated products has come into question; cautious woodworkers will want to wear dust masks when cutting treated lumber and should never, under any circumstances, burn treated scraps in a fire.

Wood Selection

Generally, the better grades of lumberyard wood will be free of major defects, but it's always a good idea to visually check the lumber that you see before you buy it. Some yards discourage such "hand-picking," but there's no point in paying for a product that isn't delivered.

Things to watch for (and avoid) in a piece of wood are sizeable knotholes, checks (splits), wane (excessively rounded edges), and warpage (either a bend or twist in the wood). If appearance is a major concern, as in hardwoods, the existence of pith, stain, or insect holes can affect your choice.

Workability of certain woods may be of some concern, but with a well-equipped workshop, this becomes less important. A dense softwood such as Southern longleaf (yellow) pine or Douglas fir will cut and work well; a wood like poplar on the other hand, tears easily and offers ragged cuts. Oaks, like most of the hardwoods, are hard on tool edges, but cut and finish well.

The choice of woods is entirely up to you. Furniture built with the common softwoods will give you a rustic look. Unfinished or surface-coated hardwoods offer a more polished, upscale appearance. Painted woods can appeal to any taste or style, and redwood makes its own statement. When all is said and done, your budget may make the final choice for you, so invest a little time (and save a little money) by shopping around before you make your choice.

PAINTS AND FINISHES

Outdoor furniture is exposed to the damaging effects of moisture, sunlight, and temperature changes. In this harsh environment, even pieces made of pressure-treated lumber—or rot-resistant woods such as cypress, redwood, and cedar—will need special protection.

Ideally, a finish should prevent excessive absorption—or loss—of moisture, while permitting the wood to "breathe." A finish should allow the wood to expand and contract, yet adhere to the grain. And it should keep bleeding and staining in check.

Finishes are used for their appearance, too. Paints can coordinate a color scheme, establish a setting, or simply brighten up dark space. A few finish coats can also be one of the least expensive coverings for wood surfaces with imperfections or poor grain quality. Finished wood is considerably easier to clean and to keep free of mildew and stains than wood left in its natural state.

Paint is the mainstay of decorating because it's available in such a broad spectrum of hues. Unfortunately, you can't always tell a paint by its color; paints vary a great deal, and it's not that difficult to select the wrong one.

Using a good exterior primer is especially important

when you're finishing outdoor furniture. Many first-time project painters skip the priming step both because painting by brush is a bother and because the finish coat looks the same whether the wood has been primed or not. This common oversight has probably caused more paint problems than all other potential mistakes combined.

A primer is an essential base coat that seals the wood's surface and controls adhesion and penetration of the subsequent coats. Primer provides a "hiding" foundation so that the finish coat will cover better, and it allows for the wood's expansion and contraction.

Choose a primer that's compatible with the paint you've selected. The two common choices are latex (or water-based) primer—which may raise the wood's grain—and alkyd, or what was once oil-based primer, which won't affect the surface and which provides excellent protection against bleeding resins. The same distinctions apply to paints as well, which is why compatibility is important.

Exterior latex paint is easy to work with, and the cleaning up process is simple. Latex paint dries quickly, resists mildew (a feature worth considering in outdoor furniture), and can be applied to a damp surface. Its emulsion is chemically less toxic than that of alkyd paint, so it's safer—and far less damaging to the environment.

Latex paint should not, however, be applied in temperatures below 50° F and should never be allowed to freeze in the can before it's used. For those concerned about the longevity of latex products, a good quality acrylic latex paint is as durable as its alkyd counterpart.

Alkyd exterior paint is simply a modern, synthesized version of old-fashioned, oil-based paints. If not thinned properly, it can be more difficult to work with than latex, and clean-up is definitely more of a challenge. Alkyd takes a long time to dry and should only be applied to a surface free of moisture. The spirits and vapors in alkyd paint are hazardous if breathed for any length of time, so if you use an alkyd paint, work outdoors. Fortunately, alkyds can be successfully applied in a wide range of temperatures.

The term "enamel" refers to a durable and usually higher-gloss finish than that of flat-sheen paints. Enamels are available as latex or alkyd paints.

If you'd like to protect your furniture while maintaining its natural appearance, a water sealer will work well. This clear wood finish soaks into the grain and protects against water absorption, mildew, and deterioration from ultraviolet light. Sealers are available as water- or oil-based products. Two coats of sealer are usually applied, the second while the first is still slightly wet. Once dried, the sealer has a flat finish which eventually weathers with age. When this happens, reapplication will provide continued protection.

A third possible finish for wood furniture is polyurethane, a clear, hard, top coating that was developed to replace difficult-to-work-with varnishes. Originally, polyurethane was recommended only for indoor use because it was susceptible to the sun's ultraviolet rays. Modern formulations have overcome that problem, but it's still important to check the label to be sure you're using an exterior-grade polyurethane. A gloss finish is likely to be more durable, but satin finishes are also made for outdoor use.

A polyurethane finish is resistant to water, alcohol, stains, and even mild abrasions. Stir—don't shake—polyurethane when you mix it, or minute bubbles will form in the blend and may not float out of the finish.

From a consumer's perspective, you might like to know that some paint and finish products are available with reduced volatile organic compounds (VOCs), the irritating and potentially harmful vapors which are released from paints at room temperatures. In the United States, California has set standards for the sale of certain specialty finishes, and some manufacturers are voluntarily marketing these low-VOC products.

If the wood with which you're working has noticeable knotholes or other surface imperfections, you'll probably want to paint the furniture rather than give it one of the clear exterior finishes. Before priming, fill the larger holes and gaps with a paste wood filler or with one of the epoxy wood putties now available. Many are water-based and stainable, which means they will take paint too. Those without zinc oxide compounds and stearates can be used under clear urethanes as well. Make sure that whatever you buy is resistant to shrinkage and can be sanded easily. (The epoxies can be drilled and shaped if needed).

No matter how you plan on finishing your furniture, you'll need a paintbrush at the very least. Go ahead and pay the difference for a high-quality, synthetic (nylon or polyester) brush. It'll hold paint better, produce less spatter, and give you a smoother finish than a bucketful of cheap brushes. A 1-1/2" or 2" trim brush should be sufficient for just about every project in this book.

TOOLS

Chances are, you already have a decent collection of woodworking tools, but you may need to do some shopping to bring your workshop up to snuff for particular projects in this book. First, refer to the list of tools given with your selected project. Then read the applicable parts of this section. Don't assume you'll need every tool we've described in these pages! And if you have a favorite tool that we've failed to mention, by all means use and enjoy it.

As you decide which tools to purchase, keep in mind that you'll be safer and happier buying the best that you can afford. Poorly made hand and power tools are cumbersome, uncomfortable to handle, and sometimes even unsafe. You can extend your budget—and your tools' life spans—by following the manufacturer's instructions for cleaning, maintenance, and repair.

Manufacturers have a vested interest in making sure that people like their products and won't get hurt using them, so spend as much time as it takes to read, understand, and remember the written directions for any tool you own. Keep the instructions handy. If you've thrown package inserts away, write to the manufacturers for new ones. Practice using new tools on scrap wood until you're comfortable handling them.

CLAMPING AND HOLDING

Clamps (or cramps, as they're sometimes called in woodworker's terms), are used to grip parts together—or to a bench—so that you can mark, drill, and glue them. Clamps and strips of wood can also be used to improvise saw and router guides or to extend the gripping surface over an enlarged area.

Many types of clamps are manufactured, but the ones you'll most likely need for these projects are C-clamps, bar or pipe clamps, and web clamps.

C-Clamps
C-clamps come in a variety of styles and sizes, but—as their name suggests—the basic "C" shape of their steel

Bar and pipe clamps

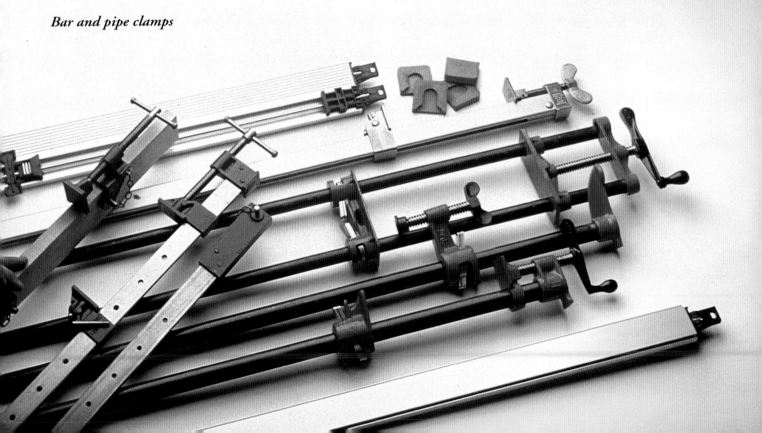

or iron frames remains consistent. One end of the "C" (the anvil) is fixed; the other is fitted with a threaded rod and swivel pad that can be drawn tightly over an area ranging from zero to several inches or more, depending upon the clamp's size. Woodworking C-clamps are usually limited to a 12" jaw opening.

Even though C-clamps can't span great distances, they're ideal for holding narrow pieces of stock together. Deep-throated C-clamps allow you to apply pressure to the work piece at some distance from its edge. C-clamps can also be used to clamp work near the edge of the bench.

Bar and Pipe Clamps

These clamps are made to span long or wide pieces of wood. The frame consists of either a steel or an aluminum bar, or a section of iron plumbing pipe several feet in length. A fixed head, equipped with a short, threaded rod and a metal pad, is mounted at one end. At the other end is a sliding tail-stop that can be locked in any position along the bar or pipe to accommodate the work.

Pipe clamps are less expensive than (but not quite as effective as) bar clamps. To keep expenses to a minimum, buy pipe clamp kits, which include only the fixtures; the pipe itself can be purchased—and the end threaded—at a local plumbing supply store.

Web or Band Clamps

Work of an irregular shape often needs a web or band clamp to hold it securely. These clamps are simply straps of woven nylon or polyethylene material that are wrapped around the work and tightened with a gripping hand-lever mechanism. They can't exert tremendous pressure, but they do fit themselves to the contour of the work piece without scratching or marring the wood.

Wooden Screw Clamps

These wooden-jawed, parallel, screw clamps are handy because they distribute pressure evenly on flat, angled, or circular work pieces. Two blocks of hardwood, each fitted with a pair of nuts, are connected by threaded spindles; each end can be tightened or loosened as needed.

Vises

A vise is nothing more than a bench-mounted clamp. It can be used to hold work pieces together or to secure

stock for cutting, filing, or mortising. A woodworker's vise differs from a utility vise in that its jaws are smooth and broad; they're usually drilled so that facings can be installed to prevent marring fine work.

Better wood vises include a dog; this is a bar that slides up from the movable jaw to hold work against a similar stop mounted on the bench itself. The dog extends the vise's effective jaw opening considerably. Some vises also make use of a half-nut to provide quick-slide opening and closing; tightening only occurs once the work is in place.

Workbench

A workbench, no matter how crude, is essential to any woodworking project. Not only is it the site for your vise, but it provides a level work surface where stock can be glued, drilled, mortised, and routed.

Generally, the heavier the workbench, the better. Even a lightweight bench needs to be sturdy, though, and a solid wooden surface is important. Workbenches of high quality will include dogs, a vise, a tool well, and stretchers between the legs for extra support.

MEASURING AND MARKING

You might think that because outdoor furniture is rugged, not as much care is required to make it. Wrong! Correctly marked and measured dimensions are important. After all, legs should be symmetrical, backs need to be even, and table surfaces are definitely more appealing when they're level.

Measuring tools establish length, width, and depth. They're useful when you purchase raw stock and absolutely necessary when you're constructing your project. Marking tools are helpful in locating holes, tenons, and mortises, and in establishing bevels and curves.

Steel Tape Measure

A steel tape measure is one of the most useful tools you can own. These roll-up rulers are made in widths between 1/4" and 1" and in lengths from 6' to 25'. The tape end has a hook that secures to one end of the work; this should be loose-mounted to compensate for the width of the hook in both inside and outside measurements.

Graduations are noted in 1/16" increments (except for the first 12", which are marked in 1/32" incre-

ments). For light carpentry and project work, a 3/4"
wide, 12' long, self-retracting rule with a tape-lock
button would be your best choice.

Straightedge

Occasionally, a straightedge comes in handy for close
measuring work. This is simply a steel ruler, 12" to 24"
long, which can be used for measuring and marking.

Try Square

This small (5-1/2" x 8") square is used to determine if a
corner is indeed perpendicular. A ruler along the edge
of the blade can be used to make quick measurements.

Combination Square

This tool can perform several functions—hence its
name. The combination square has a 12" blade fitted
with a cast handle made to slide and lock at any point
along the blade; the blade is marked in 1/16" graduations. A combination square can be used to measure
90° and 45° angles, to mark a point from an edge, or
to measure lengths. Most also come with a built-in
level and a scriber. The tool is a good substitute for
both a try square and a 45° miter square.

Framing Square

A framing square checks for 90° accuracy on a large
scale. The tool measures 16" x 24" and comes with
ruler graduations marked along its edges in 1/8" and
1/16" increments.

Sliding T-bevel

This is the standard tool for establishing bevel angles.
A steel blade pivots and slides within a wooden handle
and can be locked in any position to form an angle.
The T-bevel is used to check and transfer bevels and
mitered ends.

Compass and Dividers

A divider has a pivot at the top and two legs with
pointed ends; a compass is similar, but a pencil tip
replaces one pointed end. These tools are used to
scribe and transfer arcs, circles, and patterns during
layout.

Protractor

A woodworking protractor has a steel, semicircular
head etched with right and left 180° scales. A 6" arm,
which pivots on the head, includes a pointer that
indicates the angle when the arm is moved.

Marking or Mortise Gauge

A marking gauge consists of a block of wood with a
sliding bar through its center. The bar, which has a
scriber point at one end, can be locked at any point in
order to scribe a line parallel to any edge at which the
block is placed.

A mortise gauge works on the same principle, but
has a pair of scribers at the end (one of which is
adjustable) to mark off mortises of varying widths.
Some designs combine both tools in one.

Utility Knife

This inexpensive tool can be used to cut—as well as
scribe—lines. The best versions have retractable blades
and a blade storage pocket in the handle.

CUTTING

None of the projects in this book could be completed
without making saw cuts. Hand and power saws,
depending on their design, are capable of cutting
both straight and curved lines.

The number, pitch, bevel, and angle of the teeth on
a blade determine the saw's function. Hence, a typical
crosscut handsaw might have 10 teeth per inch (making it an 11-point saw, good for finish work). A ripsaw,
in comparison, has larger teeth and deeper gullets or
valleys; its 5 teeth and 6 points to the inch offer nearly
as fine a cut because those coarser teeth are shaped to
cut like chisels rather than knives; that's what's needed
to cut along the grain rather than through it.

Probably most, if not all, of your cutting will be done
with power saws. These often use what are known as
combination blades, which offer clean cuts both with
and against the wood's grain.

Handsaws

Crosscut Saw

A crosscut saw is, as its name implies, a saw used
to cut across or against the wood's grain. Crosscut
saws generally come in 22", 24", and 26" lengths.
They're available with 7 through 12 points per inch,
depending on how coarse or fine you wish the cut to
be. The greater the number, the smoother the cut.

Ripsaw

A ripsaw is designed to cut with or along the wood's
grain. Its length is usually 24" or 26", and it comes with
4-1/2 through 7 points per inch, the former being best

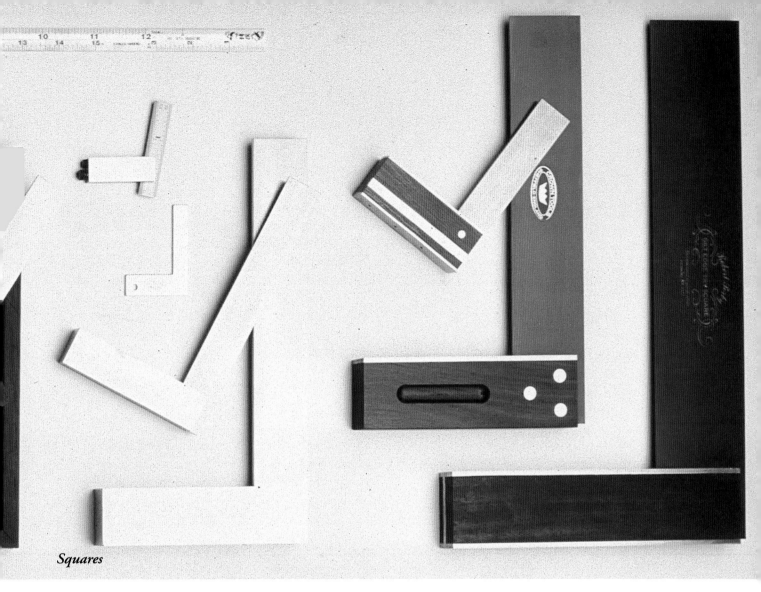

Squares

for coarse, fast cuts. If need be, you can rip with a crosscut saw, but you'll never crosscut successfully with a ripsaw.

Backsaw and Miter Box

A backsaw is sometimes called a tenon saw because it's used to cut the tenons for joints. The typical backsaw has a 12" blade with about 15 teeth per inch for producing a smooth joinery cut. The blade's back has a stiff brass or steel spine, which keeps flex in check, but which limits the depth of cut; this limitation isn't a concern for most joint-making.

A miter box can be used with a backsaw to cut miters and bevels. Economy boxes have fixed 45° and 90° angles; higher quality boxes come with saws that fit in a special jig and can be adjusted to cut any angle up to 45° to the right and left of perpendicular.

Coping Saw

This saw comes in handy for dressing up joints and for cutting curves in boards 3/4" thick or less. The coping saw's narrow, thin blade relies on the tension of a steel-bow frame to keep it tight. The blade has 10 or 12

teeth per inch, and the frame will allow a cut of up to about 6" with most designs.

Hacksaw

The hacksaw is a metal-cutting saw and is not often used in woodworking. A few of the furniture projects in this book, however, require that threaded rod be trimmed, so the saw deserves mention.

Hacksaws use 10" or 12" blades with 18, 24, or 32 teeth per inch; the coarsest cut is fine for general work. Unlike the blades in American wood-cutting saws, the hacksaw blade cuts on the forward stroke. Some hacksaws have a forward grip in addition to the handle; the grip makes the saw more comfortable to use. The better models also have a positive tensioning device and will cut in four positions.

Power Saws

Circular Saw

Hand-held and motor-driven, the circular saw may be the most popular power tool in existence. The typical saw has a 7-1/4" blade with an amperage rating (an electrical measure of horsepower) between 10 and 13 amps. The blade can be adjusted to cut at 90°, 45°, and at any position in between. When set to cut at a perpendicular, blade penetration is 2-1/4"; at 45°, it's reduced to a 1-3/4" depth.

Most better-quality circular saws come with a carbide-tipped combination blade. Tooth counts of 35 to 50 per inch are suitable for the work required by projects in this book.

Table Saw and Dado Blade

A table saw is a stationary saw built into a frame and table. This tool's weight and design allow a more accurate cut than a hand-held circular saw can deliver. Generally, table saws are equipped with a 10" carbide-tipped combination blade and have a more powerful motor than the hand-held variety. Compact and portable table saws that use smaller blades, but which have the same features as the larger models, are available.

The typical table saw has a pivoting carriage that holds the blade's arbor, or axle. This carriage construction allows the blade to be raised to a 90° cutting depth of 3-1/8"—and tilted up to 45°. (The cut at that angle is 2-1/8" deep.) Table saws also have a rip fence, which is adjustable from the right and left side of the blade. The fence guides rip cuts to assure accuracy. A miter gauge, which is adjustable to 45° on either side of a perpendicular midpoint, aids in making miter cuts by holding the stock at the correct angle as it's passed through the blade.

All modern table saws come equipped with blade guards; leave these in place while operating the tool. The guard blocks flying wood chips and helps to prevent blade "kickback," which can cause serious injury.

A dado blade is a specially designed cutting tool that is fitted to a table saw to make rabbets and dado grooves more convenient or to remove edge material in forming tenons. There are two common dado designs. One uses an offset blade that wobbles to the right and to the left as it revolves. The other design uses two outer blades and a number of inner chippers that are stacked to establish the width of the cut.

Common dado blades can make cuts between 1/4" and 13/16" in width and up to 1-1/4" in depth; blade diameters range from 6" to 10".

Jig and Sabre Saws

The hand-held jig or sabre saw is used to cut curves, shapes, and large holes in panels or boards up to 1-1/2" in thickness. Its cutting action comes from a narrow, reciprocating "bayonet" blade that completes about 3,000 strokes per minute. A shoe surrounding the blade can be tilted 45° to the right and left of perpendicular.

The best jigsaws have a variable speed control and what's referred to as an orbital blade action; this action swings the cutting edge forward into the work and back again, through the blade's up-and-down cycle. A dust blower keeps the cutting clear, and the tool may come with a circle-cutting guide and rip fence.

Band Saw

Dedicated woodworking enthusiasts hold a band saw second only to the table saw in stationary tools most frequently used in the shop. Though a band saw isn't absolutely necessary for any of the projects in this book, its ability to cut curves and circles—as well as stock

over 3" thick—makes it worth owning if you spend a lot of time working with wood.

A band saw has two (or sometimes three) wheels that guide a continuous band of steel blade within a fixed frame. The distance between the blade and frame is the throat depth; 10" or 12" is standard for most saws, with 3-wheel designs allowing considerably more clearance. A 1/3- to 3/4-horsepower motor drives the blade, which can be 1/8" to 3/4" wide and have—for wood cutting—from 4 to 12 teeth per inch.

The work is placed on a table that tilts to 45° from perpendicular for bevel cuts. A blade guide just above the work can be raised or lowered to suit the thickness of the stock being cut. A miter gauge helps in cutting bevels and angles.

DRILLING

The process of boring holes through wood requires the use of drills and bits suited for the job. Holes can be purely decorative or designed with special features such as a tapered countersink or an internal shoulder.

Hand Drills

Combination Drill
A hand-operated, combination hand-and-breast drill is an effective and inexpensive tool for making 5/16" or smaller holes, or countersink bores. The tool has a hand grip and a short hand crank that operates a gear and pinion set. For heavier work, a breast attachment can be used to apply pressure. Most use conventional Jacobs-style chucks to hold standard bits.

Brace and Bit
This tool was a mainstay of the pre-power carpenter, and many woodworkers still use it when they can. It's simply a large crank with a knob on one end, a chuck on the other, and a hand grip at the throw of the crank. It's reversible, can ratchet in both directions, and provides enough leverage to drill holes 1" and larger.

The two-jaw chuck is made to accept special square-end auger bits and screwdriver heads, though conventional bits will work if necessary.

Power Drills

3/8" and 1/2" Variable Speed and Reversible Drills
An electric drill operates more quickly and with less effort than its hand-operated relatives. For all projects in this book except the Hammock Stand, a drill with a 3/8" chuck capacity and a motor amperage of 3.5 amps or greater is sufficient. Cordless drills are appropriate for driving screws and drilling small holes, but may not be suitable for continuous, heavy-duty work.

Table saw with miter gauge

Features such as variable speed control (with which the drill trigger governs the speed of the motor from 0 to 1,100 RPM or so) and a reversible motor are well worth the few extra dollars they incur in expense.

A 1/2" reversible drill has a larger-capacity chuck than the 3/8" drill and an amperage rating of 5 amps or greater. Its motor turns at about half the speed of the smaller drill, and it comes equipped with a side handle for additional control.

Depth Control Stop Collars

These metal rings, which fit around the drill bit shafts, are used to control a bit's depth of penetration. The collars are sized to fit drill bit diameters of 1/8" to 1/2" and can be locked at any point along the shaft.

Countersinks

A countersink cuts a shallow, slope-sided hole into the surface of the work, thereby providing a nest for the head of a screw. By using a countersink, you can recess screw heads for flush mounting.

Specialty Bits

There are a variety of drill bits made to accomplish specific tasks. Forstner bits, for example, are used to drill crisp, flat-bottomed holes for fine joinery work. They are made in 1/4" to 2-1/4" diameters.

Spade bits (used with power drills) bore quickly and make moderately clean holes through wood. They're designed with a center point and two flat cutting edges and come in 1/4" to 1-1/2" diameters.

Bradpoint bits have a center point that prevents the bit from "skating" across a surface and that leaves clean sides in the hole; standard sizes range from 1/8" to 1/2".

Countersink/pilot drills combine the hole-drilling and countersinking processes in one operation. The better versions of these bits use what's known as a tapered bit, which follows the contour of a standard wood screw; they also include a stop collar. These combination bits are made for screw size Nos. 5 through 12.

Hole Saws

Hole saws are simply drum-like cutters mounted to the end of a drill shaft and equipped with a circular row of teeth at the working end. These saws come in 3/4" to 3" sizes and are generally used when the hole needed is too large to be handled by a standard drill with a specialty bit.

CHISELING AND ROUTING

Hand Chisels

Two types of chisels will be useful as you work on our projects: cabinetmaker's chisels and firmer chisels. The first type is a standard woodworking chisel used for cleaning joints, cutting mortises, and completing the general paring and shaving work required when preparing to fit wood together. A set of four or five bevel-edge chisels for hand or light mallet work, in sizes from 1/4" to 1" wide and 9" to 11" long, is sufficient. If they're to be struck with a mallet, make sure the handles are reinforced, or they may split with use.

Drill bits and depth control collars

The second type, the heavy-duty firmer (or framing) chisel, may be needed for working with large mortises. The ideal firmer has a tapered blade 6" or 8" long and 1-1/2" to 2" wide, a socketed handle, and may have straight or slightly beveled sides. It's meant to be whacked with a mallet, so it must be stout—and not too long—for control.

Routers and Bits

A router is a hand-held power tool used for cutting grooves and rabbets, shaping edges, and making slots. It allows mortise work normally done with a chisel to be completed more quickly, although corners still must be cut with a blade.

A router bit is held in a collet on the end of a shaft, which is supported by a flat base and housing, and spins between 10,000 and 22,000 RPM. The shape of the bit determines what type of cut will be made in the work, and handles on the housing allow the operator to control the direction of the bit.

The simplest routers have 3/8" collets, external clamp-depth controls, and 6-amp motors. More sophisticated models are known as plunge routers; these allow vertical entry into the work for precise cutting and have 1/2" collets, variable-speed 12- to 15-amp motors, and variable depth controls.

PLANING AND SANDING

To properly finish a piece of wood, it's often necessary to level surfaces (by removing excess material) and to make the grain smooth. Hand-held bench planes do the hard work; files and rasps cut for detail and in small areas; sandpaper prepares the wood for its final finish.

Bench Planes

The jack plane is designed for general shaving and planing work and heavy stock removal. These 14" or 15" planes have cutter blades about 2" wide. If kept sharp, and adjusted and used properly, a jack plane can produce straighter edges and smoother surfaces than machines made for these purposes.

Shorter and usually narrower than a jack plane, the lightweight 6" or 7" block plane is ideal for smoothing tight spots and small pieces of stock. Its low-angle blade, set at only 12 or 13°, allows this type of plane to be used on end grain and delicate stock.

Rasps and Files

Wood rasps are coarse-cutting tools used to make the first cut in removing wood stock for shaping or rounding. A finer cabinet rasp is made for second-cut work. Rasps come in three styles: flat on both sides, half-round on one side, and round.

Wood files are less coarse than rasps and are used for finer smoothing and finishing work. Like rasps, they're about 10" long; they usually come in round and half-round cross sections.

Sanders and Sandpaper

Hand-operated power sanders use either a continuous belt or an orbiting pad to remove excess wood. For the projects in this book, the smaller 4" or 5" orbital finishing sander is ideal. The most comfortable of these have a palm grip and either a round or square pad. The orbiting mechanism requires a 1-1/2- or 2-amp motor to be effective. For convenience, the round styles use self-adhesive paper on the pad rather than mechanical clips.

A sanding block is a good alternative to a motor-driven sander. It's a small, palm-held, hard rubber tool with a flat surface at the bottom and some type of clip mechanism at each end to keep the paper tightly in place.

Sandpaper comes in a variety of grits (or degrees of roughness): coarse (No. 60), medium (No. 100), fine (No. 150), and extra-fine (No. 220). Other grits in between are also manufactured. Standard garnet paper is suitable for woodwork and is unique in that the abrasive particles continuously break away, exposing fresh material as they do; aluminum-oxide sanding sheets, however, are more durable and less likely to clog.

WOOD JOINTS AND JOINERY

The furniture projects in this book use a combination of simple wood joints, cuts, glue, and common fastener hardware. Joints give each piece of furniture a traditional, hand-crafted look and impart structural solidity. Fasteners are used where appropriate to provide extra strength at needed junctures.

Every joint in this section can be made with one or two of the power tools reviewed earlier. Occasionally, some work with a hand tool might be needed to clean up, dress, or finish a surface.

The instructions for each project will guide you in the selection of appropriate tools. What follows here is a description of joints and fastening methods. Combine these descriptions with the woodworking techniques introduced in the next section for a thorough understanding of how the projects fit together.

JOINTS

Joints are the unions of wood used in furniture building and cabinetmaking that hold pieces together, and most are shaped and cut to serve a specific function. A joint's design gives it its name.

Half-lap

The half-lap joint is an easy-to-construct union in which wood is removed from between two, perpendicular surface cuts. Similar notches are cut in two pieces of wood, and then lapped over one another. When the intersection is kept on the same plane, the work is sometimes known as a halved cross-lap joint because only half the thickness of each piece of wood is removed to make the parts fit flush together.

Mortise and Tenon

With this classic joint, a square or rectangular peg fits into a matching hole cut into its mate. Just remember that the tenon is the peg, and the mortise is the hole. Both should be cut fairly accurately (the tenon is usually made first) because the joint holds best when it's snug.

In basic mortise and tenon joints, the tenon is centered at the end of the work piece, creating shoulders of equal width all around. Variations include the offset pattern—in which the tenon is moved to one side of the work piece's end, and one shoulder is eliminated— and the angled version, in which the piece and its tenon approach the mate and mortise at an angle; in these joints, the mortise is angled as well. Two of an angled tenon's side-shoulders (and those of its matching mortise) will be longer than the other two shoulders because of the length of the angled tenon surface.

If you have difficulty picturing this, imagine a 4 x 4 stock standing on end. If you tilt the post 45°, and then cut the bottom end at 45° to make it rest flush with the floor, the surface of the angled end will be greater than the end surface of the vertical piece. And if you cut an angled tenon on the angled end, two of its shoulders would be longer than its other two shoulders.

Dowel Joints

Dowels are wooden pins that are used with glue to hold two pieces of stock together; dowel joints join components and are made by boring one or more perfectly aligned holes in each piece of wood to be joined. The parts are then attached to each other, with each set of holes sharing a common dowel. Dowels come as rods (which can be cut to size), or as pre-cut pins. These are available with smooth sides or with ribs, the latter of which distribute glue more evenly.

Dowel jigs aid in aligning dowel holes properly by guiding a drill bit to precisely the right spot in the work. Without a jig, dowel holes can be located and marked by using a marking gauge or even a steel rule.

CUTS

Cuts are made in wood to provide a finished appearance or, much as a joint would, to allow one piece to fit inside or against another.

Dado

A dado cut is simply a slot or groove made in the surface of a piece of wood. Through dadoes are open at the ends to both edges or sides of the stock; blind dado cuts are fully contained and are similar to mortises.

A groove is the same as a dado, except that this cut is made into the side or edge of a piece of wood, usually to accept splines or to accommodate tongues cut into panels.

Rabbet

A rabbet cut is made by removing the corner from the length of an edge. Put another way, a rabbet is just a groove with one side missing. Rabbets are used on stock when pieces or panels need to be recessed so that they're flush with a frame edge; they are sometimes used for decorative purposes as well. Rabbets are cut to 90°.

Miter

A miter cut is a perpendicular saw cut made at an angle across the face of a piece of stock, against the grain, and usually at 45°. A picture frame, for example, uses miter cuts at the corners to form the joints. A compound (or bevel) miter is one in which the cut is angled across the face, but which is also made with the blade set at an angle instead of perpendicular to the face.

Bevel

Bevel cuts are made with the saw blade set at an angle other than perpendicular to the face. They differ from miters in that the cut can be made either with the grain to create a ripped bevel, or against the grain to make a straight beveled crosscut. The raised panels featured in some of our furniture projects use bevel cuts at their borders.

FASTENERS

Metal fasteners have long been used in conjunction with traditional joinery to assure the integrity of furniture joints. Small screws or finish nails, for instance, are used to supplement simple joints that would eventually separate if glue alone were applied. Sometimes, bolts are used when a piece is made to be taken apart for storage, or when additional strength is needed.

Nails

Nails are the most basic form of metal fasteners. In furniture construction, finish or wire nails are occasionally used; their narrow heads can be driven below the wood's surface with a nail set. The resulting hole is then packed with a wood filler and sanded smooth to blend with the wood around it.

Wire brads are sold in gauge thicknesses ranging from 20 to 12 gauge (about 3/64" to 7/64") and in lengths from 3/8" to 2". Finish nails come in standard penny measures from 3d to 10d—5/32" to 1/8" thick and 1-1/4" to 3" long.

Hammers for finish work, unlike the wooden or plastic-composite mallets used in chisel work, have forged steel heads, 6 or 12 ounces in weight. Cabinetmakers' hammers are ideal, though a lightweight claw hammer is also well-suited to drive finish nails.

Screws

Wood screws are perfect for drawing glued joints tightly together. Though flat head and round head screws have been a standard fixture in furniture projects for many years, the trend is now toward power-driven, flat head, square-drive or Phillips-head screws which are made to be self-tapping in softwoods. For outdoor use, deck screws are recommended; they're usually hardened and have a zinc or corrosion-resistant finish.

Generally, these screws come in sizes No. 6, No. 8, and No. 10. Lengths are from 3/4" to 3", depending upon the screw's number diameter. Finish screws are usually a square-drive design with a narrow-diameter head (less than 1/4"); their narrow holes are easily filled.

Lag screws are large fasteners used to hold heavy timber-sized pieces together. The common hex-head style comes in 1/4" to 5/8" diameters, and from 1" to 8" long, depending upon size.

Screw eyes are simply ring-headed screw fasteners which accommodate hooks or cable. They come in standard wire-gauge sizes from 3/32" to 3/8" in diameter, and from 5/8" to 3-7/8" long, with small, medium, and large eyes.

Hand-held screwdrivers come in a variety of styles for various purposes, but the most common are flat-bladed drivers with 3/16" or 1/4" blades, and the Phillips-head design in sizes No. 1, 2—and the largest—No. 3.

For power-driven screws, the best tool is a variable-speed reversible electric drill with a standard 3/8" Jacobs chuck; cordless drills will work on the smaller-diameter screws. High-speed drywall or reversible screwdrivers are also made just for fastening screws.

Bolts

Bolts are heavy-duty metal fasteners used together with flat washers and nuts to secure joints and large structural pieces. Smooth, round-headed carriage bolts are often used in large furniture construction. They come in diameters from 1/4" to 5/8" and in lengths from 3/4" to 5".

Glues

We've recommended a single glue—quick-drying epoxy-resin—for every project in this book, not because it's the only glue to use, but because we wanted to simplify the construction process and minimize your shopping trips. Made for tighter-grained oak and hardwoods, and joints with gaps that need filling as well as gluing, this two-part adhesive is our preferred choice. Standard-formula epoxy adhesives (ones that don't dry quickly) are also available and somewhat less expensive; these take 12 to 24 hours to cure completely.

If you don't mind stocking more than one type of glue, you'll want to consider two other possibilities as well. The common yellow woodworkers' glue, more accurately described as aliphatic resin, is good for holding open-grain softwoods such as pine. It dries slowly and can be diluted with water to soak more fully into the wood pores, thereby increasing strength of joints.

A second option is resorcinol resin—the only truly waterproof adhesive there is. It's used extensively in boat building and is ideal for outdoor furniture, though it's more expensive than the other glues we've described. If cost is irrelevant to you, we highly recommend it.

TECHNIQUES

This section has a twofold purpose. For woodworkers who have only basic skills, and who haven't yet learned the ins and outs of common hand and power tools, it's an ideal primer—it reviews basic working techniques and clarifies terminology and procedure.

For woodworking enthusiasts with some experience under their belts, it provides an opportunity to review techniques that are too often taken for granted and describes procedures specific to the projects in this book.

Regardless of your workshop expertise, it never hurts to have a second look at how something's done. Who knows? You may find a new twist on an old saw.

USING CLAMPS

The wood clamps used for the projects throughout this book serve the purpose of holding parts together while they're being dry-fit or while glue is setting.

The dry-fitting process works just as it sounds. After frame joints are cut, or panel tongues are cut to fit their grooves, the pieces are clamped together without glue to see if they fit properly. When they don't, wood may have to be trimmed here and there to remove a high spot or a long end.

Bar or pipe clamps are most appropriate for these oversize clamping jobs. They can stretch to match the width or height of a panel or bench back and still offer a secure grip. Dry-fitting, by the way, doesn't require a lot of pressure. In fact, exerting too much force can split a joint; all you want to do is determine whether the parts fit snugly.

For angled components such as the stretchers in the Hammock Stand, it might be difficult for a bar or pipe clamp to get a good purchase on the angled mortise and tenon joints; nonetheless, it's the tool to use. You can make it work either by setting it perpendicular to the stretcher so that it will draw against the end of the center beam, or better yet, by C-clamping a temporary wooden wedge to the angled face just over the joint and then using the flat part of the wedge as a platform to support the clamp's pad.

In the case of half-lap or other joints less than 12" in depth, a C-clamp is the universal tool of choice. You may want to cut some 2"-square pads from scrap pieces of 1/4" plywood to keep the metal from marring your work.

Web or band clamps and parallel handscrew clamps are really for special applications because they form themselves to the shape of the work. The handscrews are especially good for small-capacity (under 8" or 10") angled or broad-surface jobs, though neither one can grip with the force of a steel clamp.

The best results in joint-clamping come when you place the clamp's pressure points directly at the center-line of the work or joint to be glued. Snug-tightening is best; over-tightening can damage the wood and force enough glue from the joint to cause uneven distribution and thus a weakened joint.

How to Measure and Mark

You've probably heard the careful carpenter's slogan, "measure twice, cut once." But you can measure a number of times with the wrong tool and still come up short.

The steel tape rule is the backbone of the measuring business. With the exception of joinery work, where mortises and tenons are better scribed with a gauge, most measuring jobs fall to the steel tape because it measures quickly and accurately (within 1/16")—well enough for almost any project.

When using a tape, make sure the hook has a bit of in-and-out play, and that the tape itself isn't split near the end, where it could distort under tension and give a false reading. You can use a utility knife to mark a point, but using a V-shape pencil mark is better because the point of the "V" will always show you right where to cut.

Don't rely on a steel tape to strike a straight line, particularly over any distance. The metal band will lift or move no matter how careful you are and may literally throw you a curve. For distances less than 24", a straightedge is your best bet; you can always use the tape to mark 2' increments over greater distances, then strike lines with the straightedge if you have to.

Establishing a square or perpendicular edge is the square's job. This is necessary for marking crosscuts or for transferring a line to the remaining three sides of a beam or framing component. A try square or combination square does the task best. Rest the handle or head of the tool against the edge of the work, and mark (with a pencil) or scribe (with a point or knife) a line along the blade. To transfer the line to the other surfaces, simply "walk" the square around the work, using the tail of the previous line as the start of the next one, and so on. The combination square also includes a 45° edge in its handle; this angle can be marked on any surface.

Laying out tenons and mortises simply means planning and accurately marking their size and placement on the two pieces of stock to be joined. The simplest tool for accomplishing this is the try square, since its edge is a squaring guide and its blade has a marked rule.

To lay out a tenon, place the square at the end of the work and mark its depth on one surface. Transfer the mark, making a line on all four sides which will represent the tenon's shoulder, where the tenon meets the mortised surface. Then, with the square placed at the sides of the work, measure the intended width and length of the tenon. Make the marks, and strike parallel lines at those places between the shoulder and the end of the wood by once more placing the square against the work's end.

A beveled tenon is slightly different in that it requires two of the sides to be laid out at a 45° angle. Start by making the initial shoulder mark across what will the inside (or shortest) face. Then strike 45° lines across the two adjacent sides; these will automatically establish the position of the final shoulder line at the outside (or longest) face. To cut the inner and outer faces, the saw blade must be set at a 45° angle and the blade adjusted to maintain the 1/2" depth of cut; the teeth will have to extend about 7/8" to accomplish this. To cut the sides, the blade should be reset at perpendicular and its depth adjusted to 1/2".

Laying out a mortise is much like laying out a tenon, but you don't have to plan its depth until you're ready to drill. With the square, mark the width of the mortise at its corners (from the sides), and establish the length by striking lines straight across the surface at measured points. Mark the width lines with a straightedge or with the square's blade.

A marking or mortise gauge can be used to do the same thing, and the job may go more quickly because the scriber is built right into the tool. If the gauge doesn't have a rule on its bar, you'll still have to rely on a ruler for measurement, though.

To lay out the radius of a quarter- or half-circle, use a compass. Open its legs to the desired radius, then place the point at the center of the partial circle you wish to make, and swing the other leg to make the mark.

The same tool can be used, as well, to scribe or transfer an existing contour or pattern to another place or to a second piece of wood. Place the wood against the work you want to duplicate and follow the contour with the point of the compass, taking care to hold the tool at a perpendicular to the original face. The other leg will automatically mark the wood as you move along the edge of the contour.

You can also make a natural contour—such as the catenary curve used in making the arched back for our English Garden Bench—by using nothing more than a piece of cord. For a complete description of this process, take a look at the instructions for that project.

If you need to transfer a bevel or miter cut from an existing piece, you can use a sliding T-bevel. Its handle is placed against the edge of the work, then the blade is laid along the angled surface of the bevel or miter you wish to copy. Once you tighten the blade, it's locked, and the tool can be set against a second piece of wood while you trace the blade's angle onto the surface for cutting.

MAKING CUTS

After you've done the measuring and marking, making the cuts is simply a matter of following the instructions, but your personal safety—especially when using power tools—is a prime concern. Think about what you're going to do before you do it. Ask yourself what the consequences of each move will be before you make it! And pay attention to what you're doing while you're doing it. Sometimes the drone of a blade or the sight of it spinning through the work can be hypnotic.

Crosscuts and rip cuts are straightforward no matter what kind of saw you're using. When you start a cut with a handsaw, remember to guide the teeth with the outer edge of your thumb. A cut is always started on the upstroke, and should be made on the waste, or outer, side of the line. The blade must be kept square with the surface of the wood. With crosscuts, the tool should be held at a 45° angle; rip cuts work better at 60°. Actual cutting pressure should only be exerted on the downstroke.

When using a circular saw, make sure the blade depth is set (usually done by loosening a knob or lever and moving the shoe) so that the teeth will fully penetrate the opposite face of the work; that way, the blade will be less likely to jam. Also, make sure that your sawhorses or supports are not in the blade's path, or they'll be cut right along with your board. Draw the power cord behind you before cutting, always wear safety glasses, and sight your line of cut along the mark on the front of the saw's shoe. The safety guard will swing up by itself as you move forward.

A combination blade with a circular saw will enable you to make a rip cut or a crosscut. For the Circular Dining Table project, you'll need to cut a taper by ripping a 5" x 24" board diagonally to create two like triangles. Though this operation can be done with the help of a jig on a table saw as well, it's really easier to just use the hand-held power saw.

A table saw allows more precise cutting because it has a fence and a miter gauge. Set the cutting depth with the handwheel located at the front of the saw cabinet; the blade should penetrate the work far enough for several full teeth to be exposed; this allows the sawdust to escape and the blade to cool.

To adjust the fence, loosen the lock, and slide the fence to the right or left as needed. You can use the gauge on the fence rails for measuring the width of cut, but a more accurate method is to take a steel tape reading between the fence's edge and the tip of a blade tooth. (Pick a tooth that's set toward, not away from, the fence.) After starting the motor, allow it a few seconds to come up to speed; don't shove a piece of wood into a slowly moving blade. And don't get your hands near the spinning blade; use a push stick to pass the work through. Why? A kickback or a quick stall can put your fingers right into the saw's teeth; the work may even stay where it is.

Curve-cutting isn't difficult if you've got your line clearly marked. The thin-bladed coping saw is the basic curving tool for thinner material because it's easily controlled. If the stock is more than 3/4" in thickness, a jigsaw makes the work easier and more accurate. The tighter the curve or circle, the thinner the jigsaw blade should be so that it doesn't bind or overheat, which would warp the steel and affect the straightness of the saw kerf, or cutting slot.

Cutting at an angle can be done in several ways. If the wood is less than 6" or so in width, a miter box makes the most accurate miter cut. Held freehand, a backsaw or a larger crosscut saw can do well if the line is clearly marked.

A circular-saw shoe can be adjusted to a 45° angle for bevel cutting or compound (bevel miter) cutting. Similarly, the table saw's blade carriage can be pivoted to the same degree by using the handwheel on the side of the saw cabinet.

To bevel the end of a 4 x 4 post when making a decorative point, set the blade depth at maximum. Then mark a cut line 3/4" down from the end of the post on all four sides. With a circular saw, pass the blade through each of the four lines to remove the corners. Using a table saw, you'd remove the fence and use the miter gauge at 90° to run the post through the blade four times, rotating it with each consecutive pass.

Broad, shallow bevels, sometimes called chamfers, are cut on some of our projects' raised panels. A table saw is needed to make these bevels safely and accurately, preferably one temporarily fitted with a fine-tooth trim blade. Descriptions of how to make these cuts are included in the projects' instructions.

Rabbets and grooves can be cut with a table saw fitted with a dado blade. Remove the table insert and set the dado head width; how you do this will depend upon the blade design. The offset "wobbler" type blade has a rotating hub that changes the width by altering the degree of offset. The stacked type must be set up out of the saw and reinstalled on the arbor. When you stack the chippers between the outer blades, make sure that the teeth rest between the gullets of the adjacent blades and that the chippers are staggered around the circumference.

Adjust the depth of the blade with the handwheel and set the fence to establish the width of the rabbet as the work is passed through the saw. A stopped or blind rabbet (used in the Potting Bench project) is one in which the groove stops short of the end of the work; to make this cut accurately on a table saw, you can clamp a block of wood to the table as a stop. Establish its position by checking the work against the blade with the saw turned off. A block can be used in front of and after the blade to stop both ends of the work. For a squared stop, you'll have to clean up the groove with a chisel afterward.

Grooves for splines and tongues are cut by running the edge of the stile or frame piece through the blade after it's been adjusted for proper width and depth.

Cutting notches for half-lap joints can be done with either a circular or a table saw. With the hand-held power saw, simply lay out the borders of the notch with a square, and set the blade to the recommended depth. Cut at the border lines first, and then make several consecutive passes between the lines to remove much of the wood. The notch can be cleaned up later with a chisel.

Using the table saw, the operation is similar. Set the blade depth with the handwheel and use the miter gauge to guide the work past the blade a number of times until the material at the center of the notch is removed. A dado blade can be used to speed up the process.

To cut tenons in a large piece such as a 4 x 4, first lay out the lines, then set the circular saw to the depth of the shoulder width. (For the 2-1/2" tenons on the Hammock Stand, that depth setting would be 1/2".) Trim along the layout line and at the end of the tenon, then make the cuts in between. Repeat this on the other three faces, and finish the job by removing the scraps with a chisel so the tenons are smooth.

A beveled tenon is slightly different. It requires that two of the sides be laid out and cut at a 45° angle. This will automatically establish the position of the final shoulder line—the one furthest from the end of the tenon.

On a table saw—with or without a dado blade—tenons can be cut in much the same way you'd cut a notch, except that your cuts will be shallower, and all four surfaces will be trimmed.

Miter gauge for table saw

Stacking dado blades

For smaller tenons, you may prefer to do the work with a backsaw by first making the shoulder cuts—in a miter box if you have to—and then clamping the piece on end in a vise and sawing down to the shoulder at your marks, on four sides.

DRILLING HOLES

A wood screw hole consists of three parts: the pilot or lead hole (which is a little more than half the diameter of the screw itself), the shank hole (the same diameter as the screw), and the sink or bore, used if the screw head is to be recessed below the surface of the wood.

In softwoods, it's really only necessary to drill the pilot hole—even then, the pilot hole is sunk only a little more than half the length of the screw, to give the threads a better bite.

Very dense hardwoods and long screws may require that you drill the shank hole too. Make that hole only as deep as the shank—the unthreaded portion of the screw—is long. Note that screws driven into wood's end-grain have less than half the holding power of a screw driven perpendicular to the grain.

If you need to counterbore a hole for a washer and a bolt head or nut, use an auger or forstner bit slightly larger than the outside diameter of the washer, and recess the opening only enough to make the fastener flush. Make the counterbore hole before starting the main hole because you won't be able to center the bore point if you remove the wood core.

Combination countersink/pilot bits make hole-drilling a relatively simple task. They're sized by screw numbers, and their stop collars and countersinks are adjustable for length. Where appropriate (in softwoods, or at smaller diameters), self-tapping power-driven screws are even more convenient, though you should take care to pre-drill the pilot holes when driving screws near the end of the wood.

Drilling through-holes and bores for bolts requires

some care in not tearing out the back side of the work, especially if another piece is planned to face it. You can avoid splintering wood this way by drilling only part of the way through the piece, and then coming at the hole from the opposite side. Using a small pilot bit to penetrate the back face helps to locate the point at which to start the second bore.

A mortise is made by drilling away most of the material first, then squaring the sides of the hole with a chisel. To do this accurately, you must use a stop collar to control the depth of your bit work. Make as many bores as you can within the marked lines, since this will simplify later hand work at the sides and bottom of the mortise.

Working Grooves

Most of the joints used in these projects require that you clean up, or straighten and smooth, the surfaces which haven't been completely cut with the saw. This is a job for the chisel, and it's not a difficult one as long as you maintain the tool's sharp edge.

On some work, you may not need to use a mallet; hold the tool in your right hand to provide the driving effort, and guide the blade with the left to control direction. If you do use a mallet, strike the tool lightly so as to avoid taking big bites at once. Work with the grain, and hold the tool at a slight angle (right or left) whenever possible; this provides the smoothest cut and is less likely to dull the blade. To avoid gouging the work, don't drive the edge too steeply. Instead, hold the blade level or at a slight downward angle.

The router can accomplish quickly and more cleanly what would normally be a two-step process with the saw and chisel. For the projects in this book, as few as three router bits might be needed: a small-diameter (1/4") straight bit, a surface mortising bit (1/2" or 3/4"), and a large rabbeting bit with a guide bearing. Rabbeting bits larger than 1/2" will require a heavy-duty machine, so a dado blade may be needed in this case to finish a full 3/4" rabbet.

When operating a router, the rule of thumb is to move it from left to right; if circular or irregular cutting is required, then the motion should be counterclockwise. To avoid chipping, it's best to make any cuts across the end grain of your work before cutting with the grain.

Freehand work is fine for short jobs such as dadoes

for cross-lap joints, but when cutting long rabbets and grooves, you'll need to clamp the wood to a bench and use the tool's straight guide to keep the cut consistent. If you don't have a guide, you can usually substitute by clamping a straight section of 1 x 2 to the bench or by working along—and parallel to—the line of cut.

When edge-rabbeting for grooves, place a piece of scrap stock to the right and left of the work, flush with the working surface. These scraps will prevent the router base from tilting to one side and spoiling the cut, and will give you a place to mount a guide, as well.

Holding Things Together

The screw fasteners used in these projects don't require any special techniques other than the ability to judge when a screw is too long for its place. On joints and surfaces which are exposed or limited in their depth, allow at least 1/4" of wood beyond the point of the screw as a buffer. Power drivers can sink a screw farther and faster than you might think, and the screw's point may come through the other side, ruining your furniture's appearance or someone's clothing.

Do not over-tighten fasteners to the point of stripping screw heads or splitting the joints. The wood will swell slightly as it absorbs outdoor moisture, which will make things even tighter as time goes on.

To properly prepare for gluing, give the adhesive some time to work. Epoxy resins, in particular, need a few moments to soak into the grain, so let the glue be absorbed before joining the pieces and putting the clamps to them. Don't over-tighten clamped joints.

MOVING ON

As you select your first project, you'll notice as you scan the lists of tools, hardware, and supplies that we've included only the most important items. You can assume, for instance, that you'll almost always need measuring and marking tools, clamps, and standard items like rags and paint brushes, even if you don't find them on your project's lists.

The best way to make sure that you have what you need—and to guarantee a successfully created project—is to read the instructions thoroughly before you start. Visualize yourself completing each step, and jot down the tools that you see yourself using.

DINING OUT

Garnished green salad or chilled gazpacho, tangy barbecue or crackers and cheese, fragrant wines or glistening glasses of iced tea—whatever our concepts of fine menus may be, we all know that meals seem to improve when they're served outdoors. Fresh air lends delectable new flavors to familiar foods, and relaxing while we eat allows us to savor before we swallow. So whether you're planning on quiet dinners alone, a romantic rendezvous for two, or the annual family reunion, consider moving yourself, your guests if you have them, and your culinary choices into Mother Nature's dining room.

The tables, seats, and garden cart presented in this section will provide two special ingredients to your next fresh air dining venture—convenience and comfort. Serving is an easy matter with the garden cart—no need to make multiple trips from kitchen to table. Just wheel the cart, laden with place settings and palate-pleasing treats, from the back door to your chosen dining site. The benches and chairs are a cut above anything you might buy, and all tables are large enough to seat a family, but small enough so that a single diner will never feel lonely.

BACKLESS
BENCH

SUGGESTED TOOLS

Circular saw
Hammer
Mallet
Chisel
3/8" electric drill
Table saw (optional)

MATERIALS LIST

(1) 2" x 2" x 7' Legs
(2) 1" x 2-1/2" x 8' Skirt boards and
   corner braces
(2) 1-1/4" x 3-1/2" x 8' Seat ends,
   center divider, and seat sides
(2) 3/4" x 2" x 9' Seat slats

HARDWARE & SUPPLIES

Quick-drying epoxy resin
No. 6 x 1-1/4" deck screws
Metal angle braces
Sandpaper

Recommended Material and Finish:
   red oak and polyurethane

LEGS AND SKIRT BOARDS
(see Assembly Diagram)

1. Cut four 19" legs from the 7' section of 2" x 2" stock.

2. On the top of each leg, lay out and cut two 1/2" x 1" x 2" exposed mortises, centered 7/8" from the outside face.

3. From each of the two pieces of 1" x 2-1/2" x 8' stock, cut a 67-1/2" and a 10" skirt board.

4. On the ends of each skirt board, cut a 1/2" x 1" x 2" offset tenon, leaving a 1/2" shoulder on the bottom and a 1/2" shoulder along the front face.

5. Dry fit the legs and skirt boards, making any necessary adjustments.

6. On the leftover 2-1/2" stock, lay out four 5-1/2"-long corner braces, with 45° miters at both ends of each brace.

7. Cut these mitered braces out.

8. Apply epoxy resin to all joints on the legs and skirt boards, and assemble.

9. Attach the braces (flush with the legs' tops) with epoxy and deck screws.

SEAT
(see Assembly Diagram)

10. From each of the 1-1/4" x 3-1/2" x 8' boards, cut one 6' seat side and one 9" seat end.

11. From the remaining material, cut one 9" center divider.

12. Cut or route a 3/8" groove, 1" deep and 3/8" from the top face, along both sides of the center divider and along one side of the two seat ends.

13. At both ends of these three boards, cut a 1/2" x 1"-long x 2-1/2" tenon.

14. On a flat work surface, lay out the two 6' seat sides, the two single-groove seat ends, and the double-groove center divider.

15. Square the assembly, and mark the positions of the tenons on the seat sides.

ASSEMBLY DIAGRAM

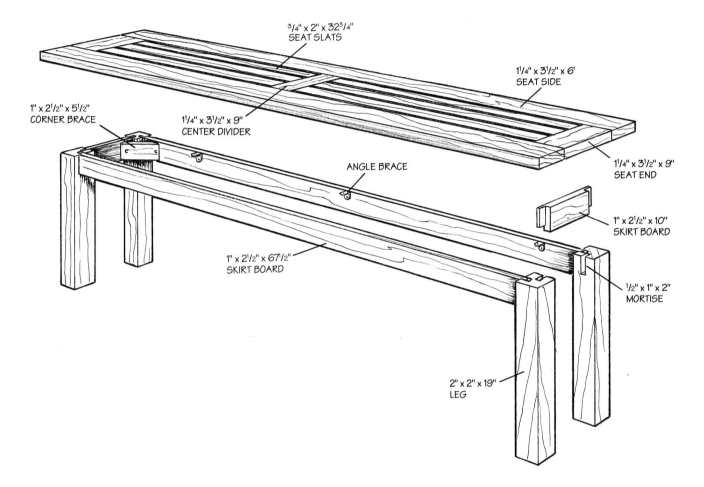

³/4" x 2" x 32³/4"
SEAT SLATS

1¹/4" x 3¹/2" x 6'
SEAT SIDE

1" x 2¹/2" x 5¹/2"
CORNER BRACE

1¹/4" x 3¹/2" x 9"
CENTER DIVIDER

ANGLE BRACE

1¹/4" x 3¹/2" x 9"
SEAT END

1" x 2¹/2" x 10"
SKIRT BOARD

1" x 2¹/2" x 67¹/2"
SKIRT BOARD

¹/2" x 1" x 2"
MORTISE

2" x 2" x 19"
LEG

16. Use a drill and chisel to cut the six corresponding 1/2" x 1" x 2-1/2" mortises at the marked locations on the seat sides.

17. Dry fit the top assembly, and make any necessary adjustments.

18. From the two 3/4" x 2" x 9' pieces of stock, cut six 32-3/4" seat slats.

19. On both ends of each slat, cut a 1" half-lap joint on the upper face.

20. Slide the slats into the grooves on the seat ends and center divider, spacing the slats about 1/4" apart.

21. Apply epoxy, and cap with the 6' seat sides.

22. Square the assembly again, and clamp it until the epoxy has dried.

23. Turn the seat face-down on a flat work surface.

24. Turn the leg assembly upside-down, and center it over the seat. Check to see that the reveal is uniform on all four sides.

25. Attach the seat to the skirt boards by fastening six or more metal angle braces around the perimeter.

26. Sand the assembled bench, and apply two or three coats of polyurethane.

35

BACKLESS BENCH

The Backless Bench is a perfect complement to the Rectangular Dining Table; in fact, its components are almost exactly the same. Don't think that these two projects are an inseparable pair, though! If you'd like to place the bench along a shaded path or by the edge of an herb garden, do. Its simple design lends itself to a variety of outdoor (and indoor) locations.

RECTANGULAR DINING TABLE

If you've ever felt ridiculous trying to serve an elegant meal on an inexpensive picnic table or on a blanket spread over the grass, you'll understand why we created this project. Designed to suggest a touch of class—without sacrificing durability—this outdoor dining table is stable but decorative, stylish but simple, sophisticated yet remarkably easy to construct. Notice that our instructions include a leg pattern modified to provide extra strength. Our original design—the one in the photograph—would have been perfectly adequate for several years of dependable use, but we wanted a table that would gracefully bear a lifetime of memories as well as a family feast.

RECTANGULAR DINING TABLE

SUGGESTED TOOLS

Circular saw
Hammer
Mallet
Chisel
3/8" electric drill
Table saw (optional)

MATERIALS LIST

(1) 2 x 4 x 12' Legs and braces
(1) 2 x 4 x 10' Legs
(2) 1" x 2-1/2" x 8' Side and end skirts
(1) 1-1/4" x 4-1/2" x 12' Frame ends
(1) 1-1/4" x 4-1/2" x 8' Frame ends
and center divider
(4) 3/4" x 2-1/2" x 14' Top slats

HARDWARE & SUPPLIES

Quick-drying epoxy resin
No. 6 x 1-1/4" deck screws
Angle braces (optional)
Sandpaper

Recommended Material and Finish:
red oak and polyurethane

CROSS SECTION

3/4" x 2¹/2" x 31¹/4"
TOP SLAT

1¹/4" x 4¹/2" x 29"
FRAME END

ANGLE BRACE

1" x 2¹/2" x 63¹/4"
SIDE SKIRT

1" x 2¹/2" x 27¹/4"
END SKIRT

1¹/2" x 3" x 29"
Leg

LEGS

(see Assembly Diagram)

1. Cut 2' from the 12' 2 x 4, and set it aside for later use.

2. Bevel one edge of the remaining section and one edge of the 10' 2 x 4 at a 45° angle so that the widest faces measure 3".

3. From the beveled stock, cut eight 29" leg halves.

4. Glue the halves together with epoxy resin to form the four legs, clamping them until the epoxy has dried.

5. Chamfer the outside corner of each glued leg 1/4".

6. Lay out and cut two 1/2" x 1" x 2" exposed mortises at the top of each assembled leg.

SKIRTS AND CORNER BRACES

(see Assembly Diagram and Bottom View)

7. Cut one 63-1/4" side skirt and one 27-1/4" end skirt from each of the two pieces of 1" x 2-1/2" stock.

8. At both ends of each skirt, cut a 1/2" x 1" x 2" offset tenon, leaving a 1/2" shoulder on the bottom and a 1/4" shoulder along the front face.

9. Dry fit the legs and skirt boards, and make any necessary adjustments. Then disassemble.

10. Rip the 2' 2 x 4 (see step 1) to a width of 2-1/2".

11. Cut four 6"-long corner braces, with 45° miters at each end, from the ripped stock.

12. Apply epoxy to the leg and skirt board joints, and reassemble.

13. Use deck screws to attach the braces flush with the tops of the legs. (Note that braces have been omitted from the Assembly Diagram.)

FRAME ENDS, CENTER DIVIDER, AND TOP SLATS

(see Assembly Diagram and Cross Section)

14. Cut two 6' frame ends from the 1-1/4" x 4-1/2" x 12' board.

15. Cut two 29" frame ends and one 29" center divider from the 1-1/4" x 4-1/2" x 8' board.

ASSEMBLY DIAGRAM

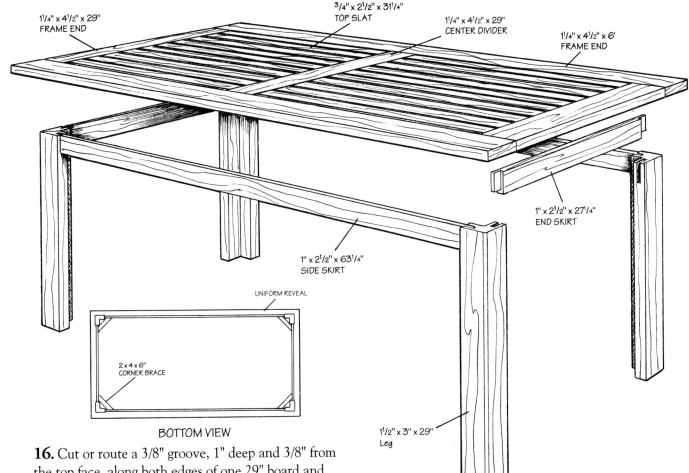

1¼" x 4½" x 29"
FRAME END

¾" x 2½" x 31¼"
TOP SLAT

1¼" x 4½" x 29"
CENTER DIVIDER

1¼" x 4½" x 6'
FRAME END

1" x 2½" x 27¼"
END SKIRT

1" x 2½" x 63¼"
SIDE SKIRT

UNIFORM REVEAL

2 x 4 x 6"
CORNER BRACE

BOTTOM VIEW

1½" x 3" x 29"
Leg

16. Cut or route a 3/8" groove, 1" deep and 3/8" from the top face, along both edges of one 29" board and along one edge of the other two.

17. At both ends of these three pieces, cut a 1/2"-thick x 1"-long x 2-1/2"-wide tenon.

18. On a flat work surface, lay out the two 6' frame ends, the two single-groove frame ends, and the double-groove center divider.

19. Square the assembly, and mark the positions of the tenons on the 6' frame ends.

20. Using a drill and chisel, cut six 1/2" x 1" x 2-1/2" mortises at the marked locations.

21. Dry fit the top assembly, and make any necessary adjustments.

22. Cut twenty 31-1/4" top slats from the four 3/4" x 2-1/2" x 14' pieces of stock.

23. Cut a half-lap joint, 1" long, across the upper face of both ends of each slat.

24. Slide the slats into the grooves on the two short frame ends and on the center divider. Space the slats equally (approximately 3/8" apart).

25. Apply epoxy to all joints, and cap with the 6' frame ends.

26. Square the table top, and clamp in position until the epoxy has dried.

ASSEMBLY
(see Assembly Diagram,
Bottom View, and Cross Section)

27. Turn the top face-down on a flat work surface.

28. Turn the leg assembly upside-down, and center it on the table top, leaving a uniform reveal around its perimeter.

29. Attach the table top to the skirt boards by driving screws at an angle through the back side of the skirt or by using metal angle braces in six or more places around the inside perimeter.

30. Finish the table by sanding and applying two or three coats of polyurethane.

Why do commercially designed picnic tables almost always look shoddy? Don't hot dogs and potato salad deserve a table just as attractive as the one you might choose for high tea or a candle-lit dinner? If someone spills the ketchup, the brightly painted surface of this eye-catching project will wipe clean in less time than it takes to throw away the used paper plates. What's more, unlike its bargain-store relatives, this table is designed to last. Just touch up its finish once every two or three years, and look forward to a lifetime of picnicking pleasure.

PAINTED
PICNIC TABLE

Circular Saw
Hammer
Mallet
Chisel
3/8" electric drill
Table saw (optional)

MATERIALS LIST

(1) 2 x 4 x 12' Legs and braces
(1) 2 x 4 x 10' Legs
(2) 1 x 6 x 8' Skirts
(1) 2 x 6 x 12' Frame ends
(1) 2 x 6 x 8' Frame ends and center divider
(4) 1 x 4 x 10' Top slats
(1) 1 x 4 x 6' Top slats

HARDWARE & SUPPLIES

Quick-drying epoxy resin
(25) No. 6 x 1-1/4" deck screws
Sandpaper
Angle braces

Recommended Material and Finish:
pressure-treated spruce, pine, or
fir with exterior primer and paint

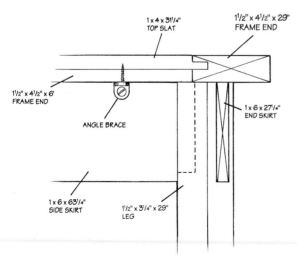

CROSS SECTION

1 x 4 x 31¼"
TOP SLAT

1½" x 4½" x 29"
FRAME END

1½" x 4½" x 6'
FRAME END

ANGLE BRACE

1 x 6 x 27¼"
END SKIRT

1 x 6 x 63¼"
SIDE SKIRT

1½" x 3¼" x 29"
LEG

LEGS
(see Assembly Diagram)

1. Cut 2' from the 12' 2 x 4, and set it aside for later use.

2. Bevel one edge of the remaining material and one edge of the 10' 2 x 4 at a 45° angle so that their widest faces measure 3-1/4".

3. From the beveled stock, cut eight 29" leg halves.

4. Glue the halves together with epoxy resin to form the four legs, inserting screws as well (three per pair of leg halves), and plugging the screw holes with putty.

5. After the epoxy and putty have dried, sand the putty smooth, and then chamfer the outside corner of each glued leg 1/4".

6. Lay out and cut two 1/2" x 1" x 5" mortises at the top of each assembled leg.

SKIRTS AND CORNER BRACES
(see Assembly Diagram and Bottom View)

7. Cut one 63-1/4" side skirt and one 27-1/4" end skirt from each of the two pieces of 1" x 6" stock.

8. At both ends of each skirt board, cut a 1/2" x 1" x 5" offset tenon, leaving a 1/2" shoulder on the bottom and a 1/4" shoulder along the front face.

9. Dry fit the legs and skirt boards, and make any necessary adjustments. Then disassemble.

10. From the 2' 2 x 4 (see step 1), cut four 6"-long corner braces with 45° miters at each end.

11. Apply epoxy to the leg and skirt board joints, and reassemble.

12. Use deck screws to attach the braces flush with the tops of the legs.

FRAME ENDS, CENTER DIVIDER, AND TOP SLATS
(see Assembly Diagram and Cross Section)

13. Rip the two 2 x 6s to a width of 4-1/2".

14. Cut two 6' frame ends from the 12' board.

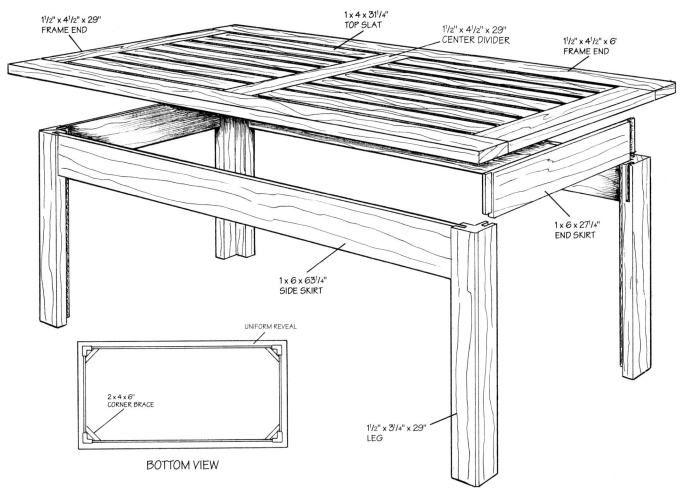

1 1/2" x 4 1/2" x 29"
FRAME END

1 x 4 x 31 1/4"
TOP SLAT

1 1/2" x 4 1/2" x 29"
CENTER DIVIDER

1 1/2" x 4 1/2" x 6'
FRAME END

1 x 6 x 27 1/4"
END SKIRT

1 x 6 x 63 1/4"
SIDE SKIRT

UNIFORM REVEAL

2 x 4 x 6"
CORNER BRACE

BOTTOM VIEW

1 1/2" x 3 1/4" x 29"
LEG

15. Cut two 29" frame ends and one 29" center divider from the 8' board.

16. Cut or route a 3/8" groove, 1" deep and 3/8" from the top face, along both edges of one 29" board and along one edge of the other two.

17. At both ends of these three pieces, cut a 1/2"-thick x 1"-long x 2-1/2"-wide tenon.

18. On a flat work surface, lay out the two 6' frame ends, the two, single-groove frame ends, and the double-groove center divider.

19. Square the assembly, and mark the positions of the tenons on the 6' frame ends.

20. Using a drill and chisel, cut six 1/2" x 1" x 2-1/2" mortises at the marked locations.

21. Dry fit the top assembly, and make any necessary adjustments.

22. Cut twelve 31-1/4" top slats from the four 1 x 4s, and two 31-1/4" top slats from the 6' 1 x 4.

23. Cut a 1" half-lap joint across the upper face of both ends of each slat.

24. Slide the slats into the grooves on the two short frame ends and on the center divider. Space the slats equally (approximately 1/2" apart).

25. Apply epoxy, and cap with the 6' frame ends.

26. Square the table top, and clamp it in position until the epoxy has dried.

ASSEMBLY
(see Assembly Diagram,
Bottom View, and Cross Section)

27. Turn the top face down on a flat work surface.

28. Turn the leg assembly upside-down, and center it on the table top, leaving a uniform reveal around its perimeter.

29. Attach the table top to the skirt boards by driving screws at an angle through the back side of the skirt or by using metal angle braces in six or more places around the inside perimeter.

30. Finish the table by sanding and applying exterior primer and two coats of exterior paint.

CIRCULAR DINING TABLE

King Arthur and his knights certainly knew about the hidden magic in circular tables, but even if you're not searching for Grail yourself, you'll appreciate this project's welcoming presence and manageable size. Made to fit into limited garden space, the table will still seat four comfortably and will look well in almost any outdoor nook or cranny. Accentuate the design of its radiating top slats by adding a Sunrise Chair or two.

CIRCULAR DINING TABLE

SUGGESTED TOOLS

Circular saw
Hammer
Chisel
3/8" electric drill
Coping saw
Jigsaw
Band saw (optional)
Table saw (optional)

MATERIALS LIST

(1) 3/4" x 3-1/2" x 10' Skirt boards
(2) 1" x 5-1/2" x 8' Legs
(1) 3/4" x 2-1/2" x 14' Top and center supports
(1) 1/4" x 3" x 2' ext. plywood Splines
(4) 3/4" x 5" x 8' Top slats
(1) 1" x 8" x 8" Center hub

HARDWARE & SUPPLIES

Quick-drying epoxy resin
(2) No. 6 x 1" deck screws
(50) No. 6 x 1-1/4" deck screws
Sandpaper

Recommended Material and Finish:
red oak and polyurethane

SKIRT BOARDS AND LEGS
(see Assembly Diagram)

1. Cut six 16-3/8" skirt boards from the 10' piece of 3/4" x 3-1/2" stock.

2. On both ends of each skirt board, cut a 1/2" x 1" x 3" tenon, leaving a 1/4" shoulder at the top and bottom and a 1/8" shoulder on each side.

3. Prepare the leg stock by ripping the two pieces of 1" x 5-1/2" material to form four 1" x 2-1/2" x 8' blanks.

4. From each blank, cut three 28-1/2" leg halves, for a total of twelve pieces.

5. Arrange the leg-halves in pairs. Along one edge of each half, cut a 1/2" x 1" x 3" mortise, 1/4" down from the top end. Locate these mortises on the edges that will accept the skirt board tenons.

6. Dry fit all joints, and make any necessary adjustments.

7. Lay the leg halves out in pairs again, with their non-mortised edges facing each other.

8. Mark and cut intersecting 30° bevels along the full lengths of each leg pair's adjoining edges.

9. Glue and clamp the leg halves together, and lay them aside to dry.

TOP SUPPORT WITH SPLINES
(see Assembly Diagram and Cross Section)

10. To save material, the six 3/4" x 2-1/2" top support pieces—with their 30° angled faces—are cut from the single piece of 3/4" x 2-1/2" x 14' stock. Lay out these six pieces so that a 20"-long edge of one piece meets the 17-7/8" short edge of the next piece; alternate short and long edges until all six pieces have been marked on the board.

11. Then set the saw blade to cut at a 30° angle, and make the first cut. Continue cutting the other pieces by turning the board end-for-end before each cut, so that you won't have to reset the angle of the blade each time.

12. Using either a hand saw or jigsaw, make a 1/4"-wide x 1"-deep groove lengthwise through the center

ASSEMBLY DIAGRAM

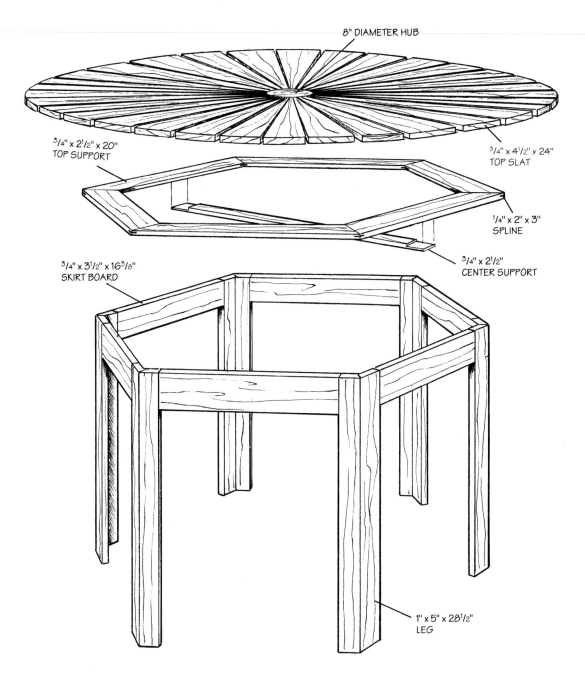

8" DIAMETER HUB

³/4" x 2¹/2" x 20"
TOP SUPPORT

³/4" x 4¹/2" x 24"
TOP SLAT

¹/4" x 2" x 3"
SPLINE

³/4" x 2¹/2"
CENTER SUPPORT

³/4" x 3¹/2" x 16³/8"
SKIRT BOARD

1" x 5" x 28¹/2"
LEG

of each angled edge.

13. Cut six 2" x 3" splines from the 1/4" plywood.

14. To check for fit, slide a spline into one of the 1/4" grooves at each intersection point, and then join the top supports to form a hexagon.

15. When the boards have been positioned accurately (opposing pairs of top supports should be equidistant), and any necessary adjustments have been made, remove the splines, apply epoxy resin to the grooves and ends of the top supports, and re-insert the splines.

16. After the epoxy has dried, trim the splines flush with the supports.

17. Glue and assemble the legs and skirt boards. Be sure to check distances between opposing pairs of skirt boards to ensure symmetry. A web clamp or tension cord can be used to hold the table in place as the epoxy dries.

CENTER SUPPORT
(see Assembly Diagram and Cross Section)

18. Measure the distance across the center of the table, from the inside face of one skirt board to the inside face of an opposite skirt board.

19. To form the center support, cut a piece of that length from the remaining 1/2" x 2-1/2" stock.

20. Place the hexagonal top support face down across the center support. Mark the position of the top supports' inner edges on the center support. Remove the top support assembly.

21. At the marked positions, cut a 1/2"-deep recess in both ends of the center support, leaving 1/4" of material. Each recess should extend from the marks to the end of the center support.

22. Fasten the center support to the top support with two 1" deck screws.

TOP SLATS AND CENTER HUB
(see Assembly Diagram and Cross Section)

23. Cut sixteen 3/4" x 5" x 24" top slat blanks from the four 8' pieces of stock.

24. Rip each blank diagonally—to make two slats per blank—so that the narrow end of each slat is 3/16" wide, and the wide end of each is 4-1/2". (Don't forget to allow for kerf when you lay out these cut lines.)

25. Use a coping saw to remove 1/2 the slat's thickness, for a distance of 1", at each slat's narrow end.

26. Lay out and cut an 8" diameter circle from the 1" x 8" x 8" stock.

27. Wrap the outer edge of the circle with masking tape, and divide the circumference into thirty-two equidistant points.

28. At each of these thirty-two points, on the edge of the circle, centered 5/8" down from the top face, drill a 3/8" hole, 1" deep. Then remove the tape.

29. Rest the hub face down on a level work surface, and insert the thirty-two top slats (also face down) into the radial holes, making sure that the slats' outer edges are equidistant.

ASSEMBLY
(see Assembly Diagram and Cross Section)

30. Place the hexagonal top-support assembly face down in the center of the radial design, and fasten each top slat to the assembly with a 1-1/4" deck screw.

31. Also insert one or two deck screws through the center support into the hub.

32. Turn the top over, and place it on the leg assembly. Fasten in place with 4-6 screws inserted between the top slats, through the top support and into the skirt boards.

33. Sand thoroughly.

34. Finish with two to three coats of polyurethane.

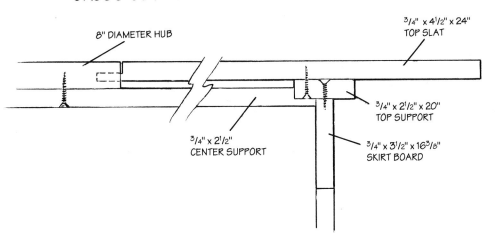

CROSS SECTION

8" DIAMETER HUB

³/₄" x 4¹/₂" x 24"
TOP SLAT

³/₄" x 2¹/₂"
CENTER SUPPORT

³/₄" x 2¹/₂" x 20"
TOP SUPPORT

³/₄" x 3¹/₂" x 16³/₈"
SKIRT BOARD

SUNRISE CHAIR

SUGGESTED TOOLS

Circular saw
Hammer
Mallet
Chisel
3/8" electric drill
Jigsaw
Band saw (optional)
Table saw (optional)

MATERIALS LIST

(1) 3/4" x 3-1/2" x 8' Seat-back rails
     and back slats
(1) 1-3/4" x 7-1/4" x 6' Back legs,
     seat rails, and stretchers
(1) 1-3/4" x 5-1/4" x 3' Front legs
     and stretchers
(2) 3/4" x 2-1/2" x 6' Seat slats

HARDWARE & SUPPLIES

Quick-drying epoxy resin
(12) 1" finishing screws
Sandpaper

Recommended Material and Finish:
red oak and polyurethane

BACK SLAT DETAIL

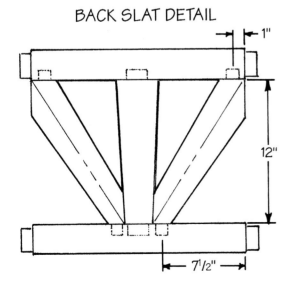

SEAT BACK RAILS
(see Assembly Diagram and Back Slat Detail)

1. From the 3/4" x 3-1/2" stock, cut a 45" section, and rip it to a width of 2-1/2".

2. From the ripped board, cut two 20-1/2" seat back rails.

3. On both ends of each rail, cut a 1/4" x 1" x 2" tenon.

4. Cut a 1/4" x 1" x 2" mortise, centered on the inside edge of each rail.

5. On the lower rail, cut two mortises along the same edge. Each should measure 1/4" x 1" x 1", and each should be centered 7-1/2" in from one end of the rail.

6. On the upper rail, cut two more 1/4" x 1" x 1" mortises, centered 1" in from each end.

SEAT BACK SLATS
(see Back Slat Detail)

7. Cut one 14" and two 16" back slats from the remaining 3-1/2" stock.

8. At each end of the 14" center slat, cut a 1/4" x 1" x 2" tenon.

9. Using a jigsaw or band saw, taper all three slats from a width of 3-1/2" at the top to 2-1/2" at the bottom.

10. Join the upper and lower rails to the center slat, and clamp the assembly to a flat work surface so that the rails are separated by a uniform distance of 12".

11. Position the two 16" slats so that their center lines intersect both the corner formed by the lower rail and center slat and the ends of the upper rail.

12. On the slats, mark the outer edges and the four tenon locations.

13. Remove the slats, cut the 1/4" x 1" x 1" tenons, and trim away the excess border material.

14. When the fit is satisfactory, glue the rails and slats together, and set them aside to dry.

LEGS, SEAT RAILS, AND STRETCHERS

(see Assembly Diagram, Mortise Guide, and Rear Leg Layout)

15. Cut the 6' length of 1-3/4" x 7-1/4" stock in half.

16. Using the illustration as a guide, lay out a back leg, a seat rail, and one seat stretcher on each of the two blanks.

17. Cut out the four pieces from each board.

18. Rip the 1-3/4" x 5-1/4" x 3' board into two 1-3/4" x 2-1/2" x 36" pieces.

19. Cut a 16-1/4" front leg from each piece.

20. Rip the remaining two pieces to a width of 1-3/4", and from each piece, cut one 15-1/8" stretcher.

21. On both ends of each of the four 1-3/4" x 1-3/4" x 15-1/8" stretchers, cut a 1/2" x 1" x 1" tenon.

ASSEMBLY DIAGRAM

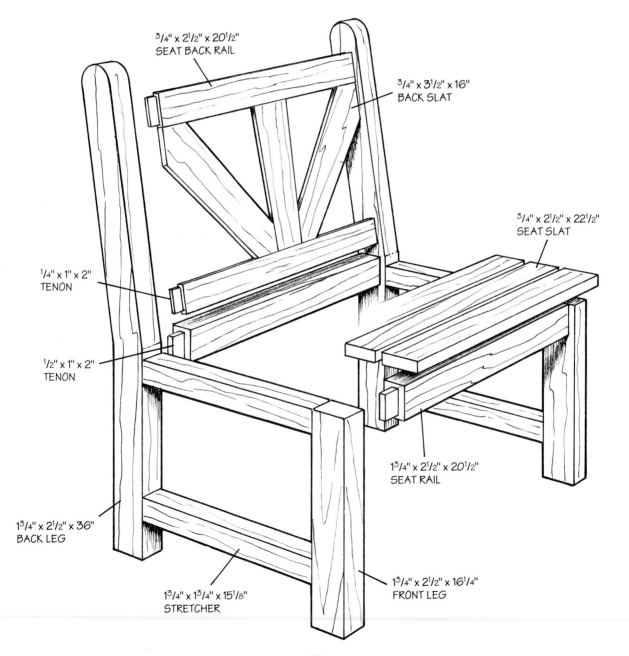

³/4" x 2¹/2" x 20¹/2"
SEAT BACK RAIL

³/4" x 3¹/2" x 16"
BACK SLAT

³/4" x 2¹/2" x 22¹/2"
SEAT SLAT

¹/4" x 1" x 2"
TENON

¹/2" x 1" x 2"
TENON

1³/4" x 2¹/2" x 20¹/2"
SEAT RAIL

1³/4" x 2¹/2" x 36"
BACK LEG

1³/4" x 1³/4" x 15¹/8"
STRETCHER

1³/4" x 2¹/2" x 16¹/4"
FRONT LEG

22. On the ends of the two 1-3/4" x 2-1/2" x 20-1/2" seat rails, cut 1/2" x 1" x 2" tenons.

23. Cut corresponding mortises in the front and back legs, using the Mortise Guide to determine placement.

24. Dry fit all joints, and make adjustments as necessary.

25. Before disassembling, measure and mark a point on the back leg 1" above the rear seat rail. The bottom of the lower seat-back rail will meet this point.

26. Place the back-slat assembly against the back legs at the appropriate height, and mark the location of the four tenons.

ASSEMBLY AND SEAT SLATS
(see Assembly Diagram and Mortise Guide)

27. Disassemble the chair, and cut the remaining four marked 1/4" x 1" x 2" mortises on the back legs.

28. Glue all the joints with epoxy resin, and clamp the chair together until the epoxy has dried.

29. From the 6' 3/4" x 2-1/2" stock, cut six 22-1/2" seat slats.

30. When the chair is dry, attach the slats to the upper stretchers with epoxy and finishing screws, leaving 1/4" between each slat, and allowing the front slat to extend 1" past the front rail.

31. Finish the chair by sanding and applying two coats of polyurethane.

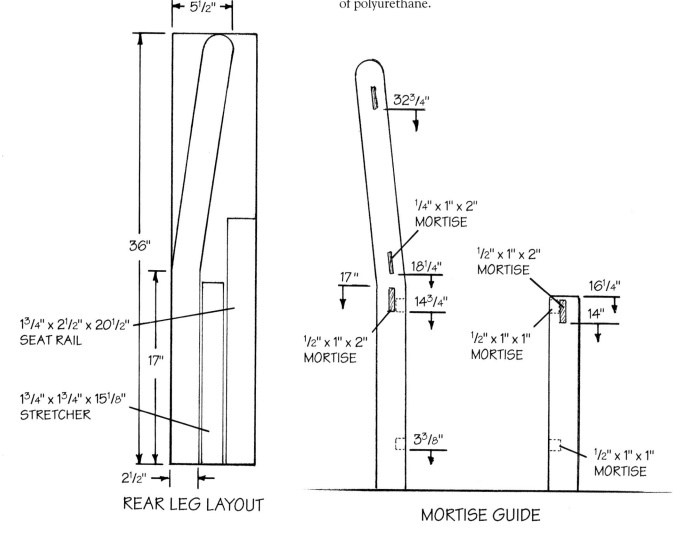

REAR LEG LAYOUT

MORTISE GUIDE

51

GARDEN CART

This versatile two-wheeled cart was originally designed as a handy mealtime wagon—a way to transport all your fixings from kitchen to picnic table and back. But for the avid gardener, it can serve as a portable worktable instead. The holes in the cart's tray will accept small clay pots or garden tools just as easily as they hold glasses, and the cart's shelves won't discriminate between platters of steaming food and bags of rich compost. Whether you're serving an outdoor banquet or bustling through spring planting season, you'll find that this cart is a marvelous time and energy saver.

GARDEN CART

SUGGESTED TOOLS

Circular saw
Hammer
Chisel
Screwdriver
3/8" electric drill
Jigsaw
Try square
Compass
Table saw with dado blade (optional)
Hole saw with 2-1/8" bore (optional)

MATERIALS LIST

(1) 2 x 10 x 8' Side handles
(1) 2 x 4 x 12' Legs
(1) 1 x 6 x 6' Cross members
(1) 3/4" x 12" x 4' ext. plywood Trays
    and wheels
(1) 2 x 4 x 10' Ledgers
(4) 1 x 4 x 8' Slats

HARDWARE & SUPPLIES

Quick-drying epoxy resin
No. 6 x 1-1/4" deck screws
No. 10 x 2-1/2" deck screws
6d finishing nails
(2) 5/8" carriage bolts with washers
(2) 5/8" nuts
Sandpaper

Recommended Material and Finish:
pressure-treated spruce, pine, or fir
with exterior primer and paint

SIDE HANDLES
(see Side Handle Layout)

1. Cut the 8' 2 x 10 into two 4' lengths to form two side handle blanks.

2. With a compass, draw a circle (4-5/8" radius) at one end of each handle. Locate its center on the handle's center line, 4-5/8" in from one end.

3. Draw another circle (2-5/8" radius) within the larger circle. Both circles should share the same center point.

4. Draw a line lengthwise down the face of each handle, 5-1/2" in from either long edge.

5. Drill a pilot hole along any inner point of each inner circle.

6. Use a jigsaw to cut out the two inner circles.

7. Also use the jigsaw to cut around the outside edges of the marked outer circles.

8. With a circular saw, rip the length of the handles along the marked 5-1/2" lines, leaving the 5-1/2" width section attached to the 9-1/4" diameter handles.

9. Using the Side Handle Layout as a placement guide, create four 3/4"-deep notches along the inner face of each side handle with either a table saw and dado blade or with a circular saw. Notches can be made quickly with a circular saw. Set the blade to the desired depth, and then carefully make the two outermost cuts on each notch. Make several more passes, 3/8" to 1/2" apart. Clean out the remaining material with a chisel.

LEGS AND CROSS MEMBERS
(see Assembly Diagram)

10. Form the four legs by cutting two 36" and two 33-1/2" lengths from the 12' 2 x 4.

11. Cut a 3/4" x 5-1/2" half-lap joint at the top of each leg's outer face.

12. To make the cross members, cut three 22-1/2" sections from the 1 x 6 x 6' board.

13. Lay the two side handles on a flat work surface with their notches facing up. Place a notched 36" leg in the 4-1/4" notch on each handle, sliding each leg forward to create a 3/4" space between the leg and the back of the notch (see upper right-hand corner of Assembly Diagram).

14. Square and secure each leg with epoxy and a No. 6 x 1-1/4" deck screw.

15. Locate the two 2 x 4 x 33-1/2" legs. On each of these legs, measure and mark a point in the center of the 3-1/2" face, 2-1/2" up from the bottom.

16. Drill a 5/8" hole through each marked point.

17. Mate the top ends of these legs to the 3-1/2" half-lap notches at the side handles' front ends. Square and secure the legs with epoxy and No. 6 x 1-1/4" deck screws.

18. Join the two side handles by inserting the three 22-1/2" cross members into the remaining 3/4" x 5-1/2" notches and securing them with epoxy and screws.

TRAYS AND LEDGERS
(see Assembly Diagram)

19. Cut a 21" section from the 12" strip of 3/4" plywood. From that section, rip two 4" x 21" trays.

20. Along the center line of one tray, cut six, evenly spaced 2-1/8" holes. (This can be accomplished quickly with a hole saw mounted on a drill or with a jigsaw. Don't hesitate to enlarge these holes to suit their intended use.)

21. Insert the solid plywood bottom tray between the two front cross members. Make sure that the tray's bottom face is flush with the lower edges of the cross members. Secure it with 6d finishing nails.

22. Slide the upper, pre-drilled tray into the same cavity, and secure it with finishing nails, 1-1/2" down from the top edge of the cross members.

23. Rip two 1-1/2" x 1-1/2" x 10' lengths from the 10' 2 x 4.

24. To form the upper ledgers, cut two, mitered 32-1/4" lengths and two, mitered 21" lengths from one of these ripped sections.

25. Place these ledgers along the cart's inside perimeter, 3" down from the top, and secure them with 2-1/2" screws inserted from the inside.

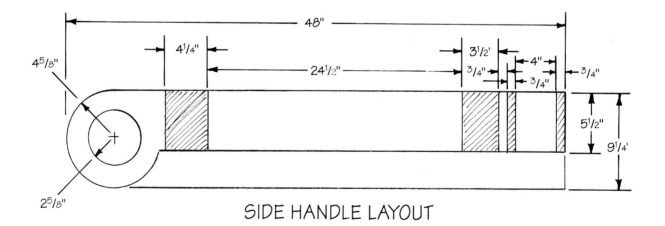

SIDE HANDLE LAYOUT

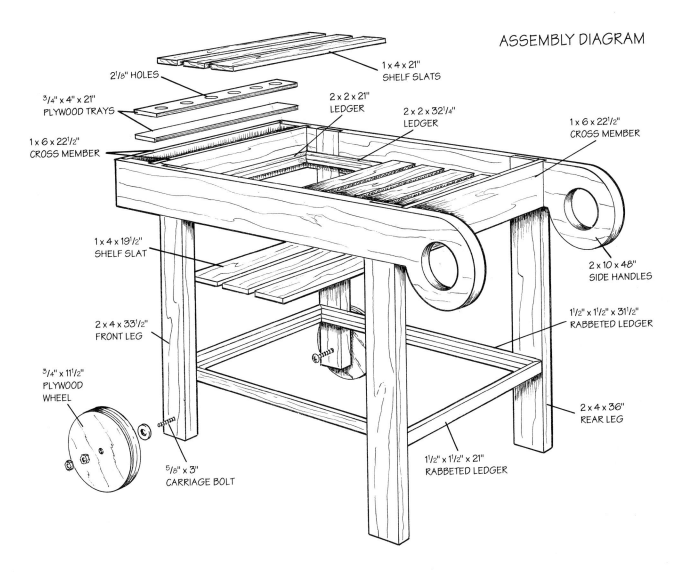

2¹/₈" HOLES

1 x 4 x 21"
SHELF SLATS

³/₄" x 4" x 21"
PLYWOOD TRAYS

2 x 2 x 21"
LEDGER

2 x 2 x 32¹/₄"
LEDGER

1 x 6 x 22¹/₂"
CROSS MEMBER

1 x 6 x 22¹/₂"
CROSS MEMBER

1 x 4 x 19¹/₂"
SHELF SLAT

2 x 10 x 48"
SIDE HANDLES

2 x 4 x 33¹/₂"
FRONT LEG

1¹/₂" x 1¹/₂" x 31¹/₂"
RABBETED LEDGER

³/₄" x 11¹/₂"
PLYWOOD
WHEEL

5/₈" x 3"
CARRIAGE BOLT

1¹/₂" x 1¹/₂" x 21"
RABBETED LEDGER

2 x 4 x 36"
REAR LEG

26. Cut a 3/4" x 3/4" rabbet along one edge of the other 1-1/2" x 1-1/2" x 10' length.

27. To form the lower ledgers, cut this piece into two, mitered 31-1/2" and two, mitered 21" lengths.

28. Using deck screws, attach the two long ledgers (with rabbets facing up and to the inside) to the inside faces of the legs, 21-3/4" below the upper ledgers.

29. Complete the lower tray by attaching the two 21" ledgers between the two pairs of front and rear legs.

SLATS AND WHEELS
(see Assembly Diagram)

30. Cut eight 21" slats from two of the four 8' 1 x 4s. Space these slats evenly across the upper ledgers, and fasten each one in place with epoxy and deck screws.

31. From the two remaining 8' 1 x 4s, cut seven 19-1/2" slats. Space these evenly within the rabbeted perimeter of the lower ledgers, and fasten each one in place with epoxy and deck screws.

32. To finish the cart, cut two 11-1/2" diameter wheels from the remaining plywood, and drill a 5/8" hole in the center of each.

33. Attach the wheels to the front legs with 5/8" carriage bolts, washers, and nuts. (If wheels of larger or smaller diameters are used, the location of the axle holes on the front legs will have to be adjusted to keep the cart level.)

34. Sand the assembled cart.

35. To finish, use an exterior primer and two or more coats of paint.

LOUNGING IN THE SUN OR SHADE

When you think about your garden, is the first image that comes to mind framed by your living room window? Or do you actually picture yourself outdoors—slavishly digging at dandelion roots and mowing the grass? Appreciating your outdoor property from a favorite armchair is one of life's greater pleasures, of course, and anyone in love with gardening knows that working outdoors can be addictive, but if these perspectives are the only two you've had recently, you're depriving yourself of a truly marvelous alternative—lounging outdoors.

We've all thought about lingering on the lawn or lazing by a favorite flower bed, but fantasies like these fade quickly when we think about hunkering down on a hard rock, damp grass, or porch step. Imagine, instead, sipping a first cup of morning coffee under the spreading branches of a favorite tree—while you sit in a comfortable Adirondack chair. Or holding hands with a loved one while you snuggle up in a porch swing. A quiet afternoon and a good book can both be enjoyed on the recliner or tree surround we've included, and if you'd like a cat-nap, what better place to take one than in a gently swaying hammock? Whether you like to daydream, doze, read, or reminisce, you'll find a project in this section to help you do it with pleasure.

HAMMOCK
STAND

SUGGESTED TOOLS

Circular saw
Mallet
Firmer chisel
1/2" reversible drill
Try square

MATERIALS LIST

(1) 4 x 4 x 16' Center beam
(1) 4 x 4 x 12' Feet and uprights
(1) 4 x 4 x 10' Stretchers

HARDWARE & SUPPLIES

Quick-drying epoxy resin
(4) 3/8" x 2-1/2" lag bolts with
    washers
(2) 3/8" x 2" screw eyes
Sandpaper

Recommended Material and Finish:
red oak and polyurethane

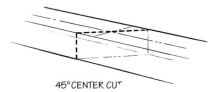

TENON CONSTRUCTION

45° CENTER CUT

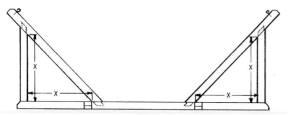

SIDE VIEW

CENTER BEAM AND FEET
(see Assembly Diagram)

1. On the top surface of the 16' 4 x 4 center beam, cut a 45° decorative bevel, approximately 1-3/4" from each end. (Lay out these bevels as 2-1/4" lengths on the flat surface of the beam.)

2. Turn the center beam over.

3. Lay out and cut two 3-1/2"-wide x 1-3/4"-deep notches, 32" in from each end. These notches are easy to make with a circular saw. Just set the blade depth at 1-3/4", and make several passes between the layout lines. Remove the remaining material with a chisel.

4. Make the feet by cutting two 36" lengths from the 14' 4 x 4 and beveling both ends of each foot.

5. Cut a 3-1/2"-wide x 1-3/4"-deep notch in the center of each. These half-laps will match the notches in the beam.

6. Check the fit of the two half-lap joints by dry fitting the feet to the center beam. Remove additional wood as necessary.

STRETCHERS AND UPRIGHTS
(see 45° Center Cut,
Tenon Construction, and Side View)

7. Lay out the 10' 4 x 4 into two equally long stretchers by drawing a 45° line through the center point of one of the four faces.

8. Use a try square to transfer this line to the opposite face.

9. Set the circular saw at full depth, and make a cut along each line to separate the two halves. Support the 4 x 4 along its full length in order to avoid pinching the saw blade. Cut a decorative bevel on the square end of each stretcher if you like.

10. Use the same layout and cutting methods to cut two 37-3/4" uprights from what remains of the 14' 4 x 4.

11. Use the try square to lay out a 2-1/2" x 2-1/2" x 2-1/2" tenon on each end of the two 37-3/4" uprights.

12. Fashion the tenons by setting the circular saw to a 1/2" depth and trimming along the layout line, along the outer edge, and several places in between. On two of the beveled ends' faces, the saw blade will have to be angled to 45°—and extended—to maintain the 1/2" depth of cut.

13. Repeat this process on the beveled ends of the two 5' stretchers.

14. Lay out two 2-1/2" x 2-1/2" x 2-1/2" mortises along the top of the center beam, 2-1/4" in from each end.

15. Remove most of the material from these mortises with the 1/2" drill and an auger bit by drilling multiple holes just shy of the trim line. Clean the remaining material out of the mortises with a firmer chisel and mallet.

16. Lay out a second set of mortises 2-1/2" wide by 3-1/2" long x 2-1/2" deep, 36-1/4" in from each end of the center beam. Rough out the pockets as before. The exact dimensions are not critical as long as the length of the upright's inner face remains equal to the horizontal distance between upright and stretcher along the top surface of the center beam (see Side View).

17. Cut a similar mortise on the inner (lower) face of each stretcher, 31" up from the angled tenon. (Don't be disturbed by the difference between some mortise measurements and the measurements of their partner tenons! The measurement of the angled surface of a tenon is always greater than its layout measurement on a flat surface. Mortises are therefore cut to accommodate this increased tenon surface.)

18. Dry fit the entire assembly, and make adjustments as necessary.

19. Remove the uprights and stretchers, and turn the center beam upside-down.

20. At each half-lap joint, drill two 1-1/2" diameter holes approximately 1/2" deep. With a 1/4" bit, drill down another 2" at the center of each hole.

ASSEMBLY
(see Assembly Diagram)

21. Fasten the feet to the center beam by inserting four 3/8" x 2-1/2" lag bolts with washers through the countersunk holes.

22. Turn the center assembly over, and glue the uprights and stretchers in place with epoxy.

23. Attach a 3/8" x 2" screw eye approximately 3-1/2" down from the top of each stretcher. This position may be adjusted according to the size of your hammock.

24. The completed stand should be sanded and finished with polyurethane.

ASSEMBLY DIAGRAM

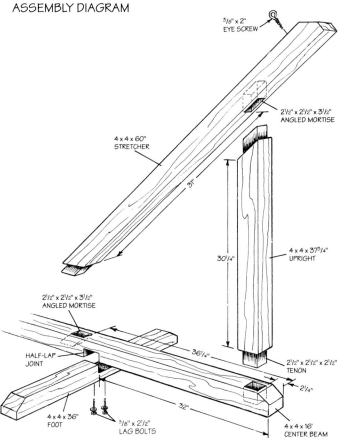

59

HAMMOCK STAND

Tired of wishing that someone had planted those two hammock-hanging trees for you thirty years ago? Wish no more. If your garden offers a sixteen-foot-long stretch of level ground, this hammock stand belongs on it. Simple in design, but just as stable as those trees you thought you needed, the stand can be located in sun or shade and can be adjusted to accommodate hammocks of almost any size.

RECLINER

Is relaxing in the yard one of your everyday activities, or are you so driven by the demands of daily life that even the thought of slowing down fosters guilt? If you haven't yet realized how glorious it feels—and how healthy it is—to do absolutely nothing outdoors, this project is for you. You can satisfy your compulsive need to work by building it—and then luxuriate in the results!

RECLINER

SUGGESTED TOOLS

Circular saw
Hammer
Chisel
3/8" electric drill
Jigsaw
Router
Table saw (optional)
Band saw (optional)

MATERIALS LIST

(1) 2 x 4 x 14' Side rails
(3) 2 x 4 x 16' Legs, stretchers, seat
   back frame, props, and slats

HARDWARE & SUPPLIES

(6) 5/8" finishing screws
Sandpaper
Quick-drying epoxy resin
(8) No. 6 x 1-1/4" deck screws
(2) 3/8" x 2-1/2" lag screws
4" of 7/16" dowel

Recommended Material and Finish:
   redwood and water sealer

SIDE RAILS, LEGS, AND STRETCHERS
(see Assembly Diagram)

1. Form the side rails by cutting the 14' 2 x 4 into two 7' sections.

2. Set your router bit or dado blade to cut a 1/2" x 1/2" groove.

3. Choose the best face of each rail.

4. On the opposite face, lay out and cut a 57-1/2"-long, 1/2" x 1/2" groove, 1/4" down from the rail's top. Start this groove 1-1/2" in from one end of each rail, and stop it 25" in from the other end.

5. On the bottom edge of each rail, 12" in from each end, lay out and cut two 1/2" x 2"-deep x 2-1/2" mortises.

6. Cut four 10-1/2" legs from one of the 16' 2 x 4s.

7. On the top end of each leg, cut a 1/2" x 2" x 2-1/2" tenon.

8. With a jigsaw or band saw, round off the bottom of each leg by cutting a 3-1/2" diameter semicircle.

ASSEMBLY DIAGRAM

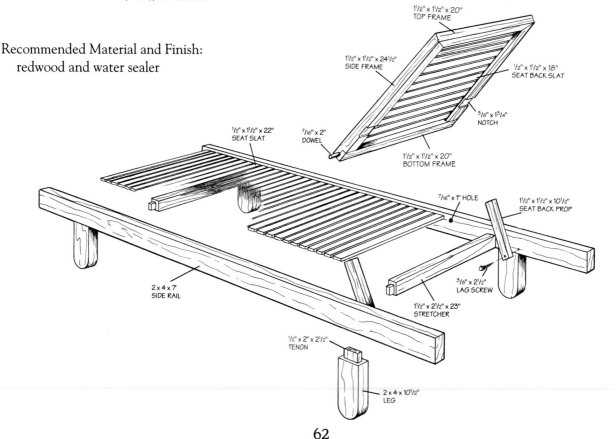

62

9. Cut two 23"-long stretcher blanks from the same 2 x 4.

10. Rip the blanks down to 2-1/2" in width.

11. On both ends of the two stretchers, lay out and cut a 1/2" x 1-1/2" x 1"-long tenon.

12. Lay out two corresponding mortises on the inside faces of each side rail, 16" in from each end and 1/2" up from the bottom edge.

13. Dry fit the rails, stretchers, and legs, making adjustments as necessary.

SEAT BACK FRAME AND SLATS
(see Assembly Diagram)

14. Cut another section, 5' long, from the 2 x 4.

15. Rip this section twice to yield two 1-1/2" x 1-1/2" x 5' pieces of stock.

16. From each of these pieces, cut a 20" frame and a 24-1/2" frame.

17. To shape the 20" top frame, cut a 45° miter on each end (see Assembly Diagram).

18. Shape the two 24-1/2" side frames by cutting 45° miters on their top ends only.

19. Using a router or dado blade, form a 1/2" x 1/2" groove along the inner edges of the two 24-1/2" side frames. Locate these grooves 1/4" down from the upper face, just as you did with the grooves on the side rails.

20. Lay out and cut a 3/8" x 1-3/4" notch on the back of each side frame, centered 8-3/8" up from the bottom end.

21. On a flat work surface, lay out the pieces to form a rectangle, and square the corners.

22. Mark and cut two half-lap joints at the bottom of each side frame and at both ends of the bottom frame (see Assembly Diagram).

23. Fasten the frame together with finishing screws (not glue), being careful not to position screws where they will interfere with the dowel hole you'll be creating in step 24.

24. Into the outer edge of each side frame, drill a 7/16" hole, 1/2" deep and 3/4" up from the bottom edge.

25. In each side rail, drill a corresponding 1"-deep hole, 3/4" down from the top face and 1" from the end of the 1/2" x 1/2" groove.

26. Rip the remaining two 16' 2 x 4s into 1/2" x 1-1/2" strips. Each board should yield four strips.

27. Cut thirty-two 22" seat slats and twelve 18" seat back slats from these strips.

ASSEMBLY AND PROPS
(see Assembly Diagram)

28. Sand all pieces well.

29. Remove the finishing screws in the mitered top frame of the seat back, and remove the top frame piece.

30. Insert the seat back slats between the side frames, spacing them at an equal distance from one another.

31. Glue the slats in place, and replace the top frame and screws.

32. Apply epoxy to two 2" dowels, and insert them into the side frames' holes.

33. Assembly of the side rails, stretchers, seat back, and seat slats will require some forethought and a bit of juggling. The dowels in the framed back must be inserted (without epoxy) into the rails' holes as (not after) the seat slats are spaced and glued with epoxy into the rails' grooves. Make sure that the slats are equally spaced and that the dowels are free to move.

34. When the epoxy has dried, turn the recliner over, and attach the legs, also with epoxy. For additional support, 1-1/4" screws can be installed from the inside face.

35. Turn the recliner right-side up.

36. Cut two 10-1/2" seat-back props from the leftover 1-1/2" x 1-1/2" stock.

37. In each prop, drill a 1/8" hole, 3/4" in from one end (see Assembly Diagram).

38. Drill a corresponding hole along the inside face of each side rail, 11-1/2" in from the end and 3/4" from the bottom edge.

39. Attach the props with lag screws, leaving them loose enough to swivel freely.

40. Finish the recliner with a colorless sealer.

STANDARD
ADIRONDACK CHAIR

The time-honored Adirondack style carries with it gentle hints of cool mountain breezes, gracious summer homes, and long, lazy vacations. This standard Adirondack chair is no exception. Its arms are wide enough to support the extras that tend to follow us outdoors: an iced drink, a book, sunglasses, or perhaps a towel. And the curved-top slats add a special, decorative touch.

STANDARD ADIRONDACK CHAIR

SUGGESTED TOOLS

Circular saw
Hammer
Level
Screwdriver
Jigsaw
Band saw (optional)
Table saw (optional)

MATERIALS LIST

(1) 3/4" x 7-1/4" x 12' Seat slats and seat back slats
(1) 1" x 5-1/2" x 12' Arms, back legs, and skirt
(1) 1" x 3-1/2" x 12' Front legs, arm supports, and cleats

HARDWARE & SUPPLIES

Sandpaper
Quick-drying epoxy resin
(30) No. 6 x 1-1/4" deck screws
6d finishing nails

Recommended Material and Finish: pressure-treated spruce, pine, or fir with exterior primer and paint

PATTERNS, SEAT BACK SLATS, AND SEAT SLATS

(see Assembly Diagram and Component Layout)

1. Begin by cutting a complete set of patterns from cardboard or thin plywood, using the illustrations as a guide.

2. Cut a 36" center seat-back slat blank from the 12' length of 3/4" x 7-1/4" stock, and set it aside for later use.

3. Rip two 3-1/2"-wide boards from the remaining 9' piece of stock.

4. From one of the two 9' boards, cut a 33" seat-back slat blank, a 30" seat-back slat blank, a 22" rear seat slat, and a 21-1/2" front seat slat.

5. From the other 9' piece, cut two 22" seat slats, a 30" seat-back slat blank, and a 33" seat-back slat blank.

6. Trace the back slat patterns onto the blanks, and cut the pieces with a jigsaw or band saw.

ARMS, FRONT SKIRT BOARD, AND BACK LEGS

(see Assembly Diagram and Component Layout)

7. From the 1" x 5-1/2" x 12' board, cut two 32" arm blanks and a 21-1/2" front skirt board.

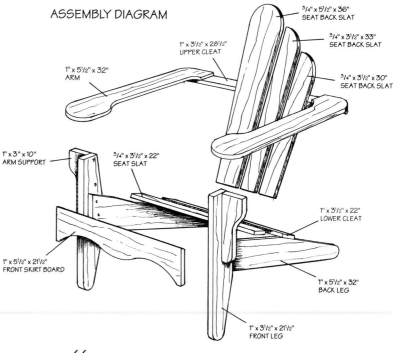

ASSEMBLY DIAGRAM

³/₄" x 5¹/₂" x 36"
SEAT BACK SLAT

³/₄" x 3¹/₂" x 33"
SEAT BACK SLAT

1" x 3¹/₂" x 28¹/₂"
UPPER CLEAT

³/₄" x 3¹/₂" x 30"
SEAT BACK SLAT

1" x 5¹/₂" x 32"
ARM

1" x 3" x 10"
ARM SUPPORT

³/₄" x 3¹/₂" x 22"
SEAT SLAT

1" x 3¹/₂" x 22"
LOWER CLEAT

1" x 5¹/₂" x 21¹/₂"
FRONT SKIRT BOARD

1" x 5¹/₂" x 32"
BACK LEG

1" x 3¹/₂" x 21¹/₂"
FRONT LEG

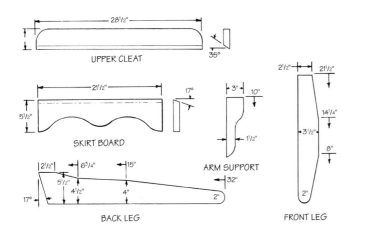

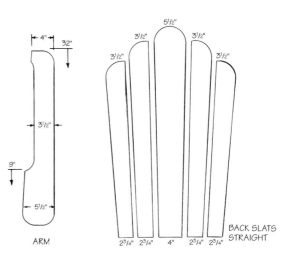

8. Overlap the back leg patterns in order to transfer and cut two 32" back leg blanks from the remaining material.

9. Transfer and cut the patterns for the arms, front skirt board, and back legs.

FRONT LEGS, ARM SUPPORTS, UPPER CLEAT, AND LOWER CLEAT
(see Assembly Diagram and Component Layout)

10. From the 1" x 3-1/2" x 10' board, cut two 21-1/2" front leg blanks, two 10" arm support blanks, a 28-1/2" upper cleat blank, and a 22" lower cleat.

11. Rip a 2-1/2" piece from the remaining material, and cut a 20"-long seat back cleat (not pictured in the Assembly Diagram) from it.

12. Cut the blanks using the patterns as guides. Make sure that the front edge of the upper cleat is beveled at an angle of 35° to conform to the angled back slats.

ASSEMBLY
(see Assembly Diagram)

13. Sand the finished components, and clear a work surface.

14. Attach each back leg to a front leg, 15-1/4" up from the bottom of each front leg and 1" in from its front edge, using epoxy and screws. Be sure to assemble the leg pairs as mirror images of one another.

15. Attach the skirt board to the leg assemblies, locating its exposed face flush with the front legs' front edges.

16. Clamp a temporary 19-1/2" spacer between the tips of the back legs to keep them from separating.

17. Fasten the arms to the top of the beveled upper cleat, maintaining an equal separation between the arms' inner edges.

18. Fasten the lower cleat to the top of the back legs, so that its front edge is 16" from the front skirt board's outer face. Remove the spacer.

19. Place the center back slat so that its back face rests against the front edge of the lower cleat. Center the slat, and attach it with a screw.

20. Position the arm assembly on top of the front legs. Allow it to extend beyond each front leg and to hang over the outside of each leg by at least 3".

21. Level the arm assembly front to back, and secure it by driving a screw through the center seat-back slat into the upper cleat.

22. Use screws to attach the arm supports to the front legs' outer faces, 1-1/2" back from the legs' front edges.

23. Then attach the arms to the supports, also with screws.

24. Attach the remaining four back slats to the upper and lower cleats.

25. To provide additional support for the seat back slats, center the 20" seat back cleat across the back of the slats, and use deck screws to attach it about 8" down from the top of the longest slat.

26. Use 6d finishing nails to fasten the front (21-1/2") and rear seat slats to the back legs. (Note that the front seat slat fits between the front legs, and the rear slat's back edge rests against the back slats' faces.)

27. Fasten the two remaining slats along the seat contour.

28. Finish the assembled chair by applying one coat of primer and two coats of exterior paint.

67

CURVED-BACK ADIRONDACK CHAIR WITH OTTOMAN

In this two-part project, we've taken the standard Adirondack Chair design and added two components: a curved back for additional comfort and an attractive ottoman for your legs. Build the Painted Coffee Table too, and you'll have a complete ensemble for the yard or deck.

CURVED-BACK ADIRONDACK CHAIR WITH OTTOMAN

SUGGESTED TOOLS

Circular saw
Hammer
Level
Screwdriver
Jigsaw
Band saw (optional)
Table saw (optional)

MATERIALS LIST

(1) 3/4" x 7-1/4" x 12' Center seat-back slat and ottoman slats
(1) 3/4" x 7-1/4" x 10' Seat slats and seat back slats
(1) 1" x 5-1/2" x 12' Arms, back legs, and front skirt board
(1) 1" x 5-1/2" x 10' Front legs, back legs, and ottoman skirt board
(1) 1" x 3-1/2" x 10' Front legs, arm supports, and cleats

HARDWARE & SUPPLIES

Sandpaper
Quick-drying epoxy resin
(30) No. 6 x 1-1/4" deck screws
6d finishing nails

Recommended Material and Finish:
pressure-treated spruce, pine, or
fir with exterior primer and paint

PATTERNS, SEAT BACK SLATS, OTTOMAN SLATS, AND SEAT SLATS

(see Assembly Diagram and Component Layout)

1. Begin by cutting a complete set of patterns from cardboard or thin plywood, using the illustrations as a guide.

2. Cut a 36" blank from the 3/4" x 7-1/4" x 12' stock. Set it aside for later use as a center seat-back slat.

3. Rip the remaining 9' piece and the other 10' section of 3/4" x 7-1/4" stock into four 3-1/2"-wide boards.

4. From each of the two 9' boards, cut three 24" ottoman slats. Then cut one additional ottoman slat from the leftover material.

5. From one of the 10' pieces, cut a 22" rear seat-slat blank, a 30" seat-back slat blank, and two 33" seat-back slat blanks.

6. From the other 10' piece of ripped stock, cut three 22" seat slats, a 21-1/2" front seat slat, and a 30" seat-back slat blank.

7. Trace the back slat patterns onto the five blanks, and cut the pieces with a jigsaw or band saw. Also transfer the rear seat-slat pattern to its 22" blank, and cut it.

ARMS, SKIRT BOARD, AND BACK LEGS

(see Assembly Diagram and Component Layout)

8. From the 1" x 5-1/2" x 12' board, cut two 32" arm blanks and a 21-1/2" front skirt board.

9. Overlap the back leg patterns in order to transfer and cut two 32" back leg blanks from the remaining material.

10. Transfer and cut the arm, back leg, and skirt board patterns.

BACK LEGS, FRONT LEGS, ARM SUPPORTS, SKIRT BOARD, UPPER AND LOWER CLEATS

(see Assembly Diagram and Component Layout)

11. From the 1" x 5-1/2" x 10' stock, cut two more 32" back leg blanks, overlapping the patterns to save material. Also cut two 17" ottoman leg blanks and a 22" ottoman skirt board.

12. Finish-cut the legs and skirt board, using the patterns as guides.

13. Cut the 1" x 3-1/2" x 10' stock into two 21-1/2" front leg blanks, two 10" arm support blanks, a 28-1/2" upper cleat blank, and a 22" lower cleat blank.

14. Again, finish-cut the blanks, making sure that the front edge of the upper cleat is bevelled at an angle of 35˚ to conform to the angled back slats.

ASSEMBLY
(see Assembly Diagram)

15. Sand the finished components, and clear a work surface.

16. Use epoxy and screws to attach each of the chair's back legs to a 21-1/2" front leg, 15-1/4" up from the bottom of each front leg and 1" in from its front edge. Be sure to assemble the leg pairs as mirror images of one another.

17. Attach the 21-1/2" front skirt board to these leg assemblies, placing it so that its exposed face is flush with the front legs' front edges.

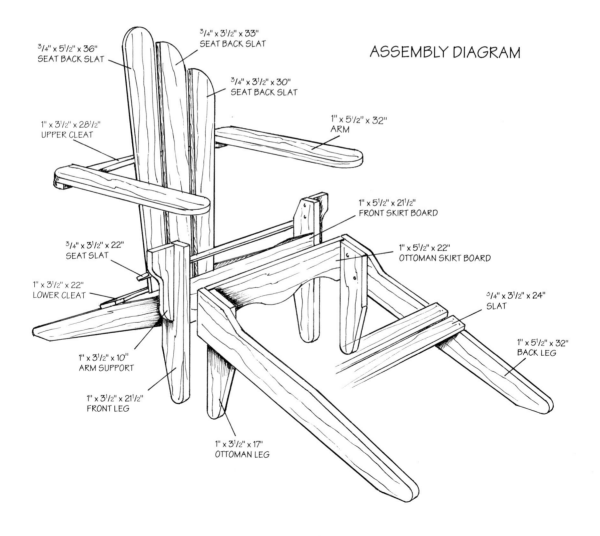

ASSEMBLY DIAGRAM

³/4" x 5¹/2" x 36"
SEAT BACK SLAT

³/4" x 3¹/2" x 33"
SEAT BACK SLAT

³/4" x 3¹/2" x 30"
SEAT BACK SLAT

1" x 5¹/2" x 32"
ARM

1" x 3¹/2" x 28¹/2"
UPPER CLEAT

1" x 5¹/2" x 21¹/2"
FRONT SKIRT BOARD

³/4" x 3¹/2" x 22"
SEAT SLAT

1" x 5¹/2" x 22"
OTTOMAN SKIRT BOARD

1" x 3¹/2" x 22"
LOWER CLEAT

³/4" x 3¹/2" x 24"
SLAT

1" x 5¹/2" x 32"
BACK LEG

1" x 3¹/2" x 10"
ARM SUPPORT

1" x 3¹/2" x 21¹/2"
FRONT LEG

1" x 3¹/2" x 17"
OTTOMAN LEG

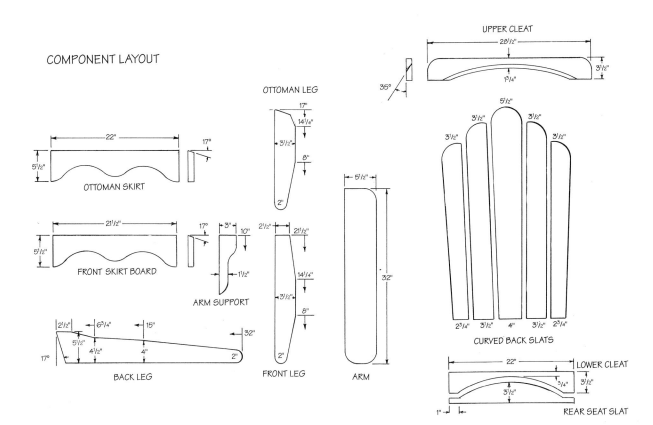

COMPONENT LAYOUT

UPPER CLEAT

OTTOMAN LEG

OTTOMAN SKIRT

FRONT SKIRT BOARD

ARM SUPPORT

BACK LEG

FRONT LEG

ARM

CURVED BACK SLATS

LOWER CLEAT

REAR SEAT SLAT

18. Clamp a temporary 19-1/2" spacer between the tips of the back legs to keep them from separating.

19. Repeat this process with the ottoman legs and 22" skirt board, but this time, hold the front legs to the inside of and 1" back from the back legs' edges.

20. Complete the ottoman by fastening its 24" slats in place with epoxy and finishing nails. First fasten the lowest slat, with its lowest edge about 5" up from the end of the leg. Fasten the highest slat next, so that its front edge is flush with the skirt board's face. Then attach the other five slats, spacing them at equal distances from one another.

21. Fasten the chair arms to the top of the contoured upper cleat, maintaining an even separation between the arms' inner edges.

22. Fasten the lower cleat to the top of the back legs, so that its front edge (measured where that edge rests on the back leg) is about 16" from the front skirt board's outer face. Remove the spacer.

23. Place the center seat-back slat against the front, contoured edge of the lower cleat. Center the slat, and attach it with a screw.

24. Position the arm assembly on the front legs, allowing the arms to extend beyond each front leg, and to hang over each front leg by at least 3" to the outside.

25. Level the arm assembly front to back, and secure it with a screw driven through the center seat-back slat into the upper cleat.

26. Position the arm supports on the outer faces of the front legs, 1-1/2" back from the legs' front edges. Attach with screws.

27. Then attach the arms to the supports, also with screws.

28. Attach the remaining four seat-back slats to the upper and lower cleats.

29. Use 6d finishing nails to fasten the 21-1/2" front seat slat to the back legs (between the front legs). Then attach the contoured rear seat-slat to the back legs so that its back edge is against the front faces of the seat back slats.

30. Fasten the three remaining slats along the back legs.

31. Finish the chair by applying one coat of primer and two coats of exterior paint.

PAINTED
COFFEE TABLE

Though it was specifically designed to complete our Curved-Back Adirondack Chair and Ottoman ensemble (all the heights match), this coffee table is suitable for any number of outdoor settings. It's light enough to move easily, strong enough to last a lifetime, and not at all difficult to construct. And remember, you don't have to paint this table—or any other project—just because we do. Clear finishes are perfectly acceptable, as long as you've selected an appropriate wood.

PAINTED
COFFEE TABLE

SUGGESTED TOOLS

Circular saw
Hammer
Chisel
3/8" electric drill
Table saw with dado blade (optional)

MATERIALS LIST

(1) 2 x 4 x 12' Skirt boards, one half-
    leg, and supports
(1) 2 x 4 x 10' Legs and corner braces
(2) 1 x 4 x 8' Top slats

HARDWARE & SUPPLIES

Quick-drying epoxy resin
(30) No. 6 x 1-1/4" deck screws
6d finishing nails
Sandpaper

Recommended Material and Finish:
  pressure-treated spruce, pine, or fir
  with exterior primer and paint

CONSTRUCTION PROCEDURE
(see Assembly Diagram)

1. Begin by cutting a 4' section from the 12' 2 x 4.

2. Rip two 1-1/2" x 1-1/2" pieces from this section.

3. Rip the remaining 8' and 10' lengths of 2 x 4 stock down to a width of 3".

4. Cut four 19-1/2" skirt boards from the 8' piece.

5. Form one of the leg halves by cutting the remaining 17-1/2" piece to a length of 15-1/2".

6. Cut the other seven 15-1/2" leg halves from the 10' length of 1-1/2" x 3" stock.

7. Along the top of one edge of each leg half, cut a 1/2" x 1" x 2-1/2" exposed mortise.

8. Cut a corresponding tenon on each end of the four skirt boards, leaving a 1/2" shoulder along the bottom edge.

9. Dry fit the components, and make adjustments as necessary.

10. Rip a 45° bevel along the non-mortised side of each leg half so that the wide face measures 3". Make sure that four halves are cut as mirror images of the other four.

11. Using epoxy resin and deck screws, fasten the leg halves together as pairs. (Fill screw holes with wood putty before painting.)

12. From some of the leftover 1-1/2" x 3" stock, cut four triangular corner braces measuring 5" along the hypotenuse.

13. Pre-drill 1/8" holes approximately 1" from the tips of each brace.

14. Assemble the legs and skirt boards with epoxy resin.

15. With deck screws, fasten the braces into the corners of the assembly. (Use a piece of 2 x 4 stock as a gauge to hold the braces 1-1/2" from the skirt boards' top edges.)

16. While the assembly is drying, cut four 20-1/2" supports—each with mitered ends—from the 1-1/2" x 1-1/2" x 4' boards.

ASSEMBLY DIAGRAM

3/4" x 3 1/4" x 24"
TOP SLAT

1 1/2" x 1 1/2" x 20 1/2"
SUPPORT

3 1/2" x 3 1/2"
CORNER BRACE

45° MITER

1 1/2" x 3" x 19 1/2"
SKIRT BOARD

1 1/2" x 3" x 15 1/2"
LEG

17. Rip the two 8' 1 x 4s to a width of 3-1/4".

18. Cut seven 24" top slats from this sized stock.

19. Use deck screws to secure the mitered supports to the base assembly, allowing them to rest on top of the corner braces.

20. Lay the seven top slats across the skirt boards, and space them equally, leaving a 1/4" reveal around the perimeter.

21. Face-nail the slats to the supports with 6d finishing nails.

22. Sand the table well.

23. Finish the table by applying an exterior primer and two coats of exterior paint.

SWING

SUGGESTED TOOLS

Circular saw
Hammer
Mallet
Chisel
3/8" electric drill
Jigsaw
Band saw (optional)
Table saw (optional)

MATERIALS LIST

(1) 1-7/8" x 5-1/2" x 11' Uprights, rails, and arms
(1) 1-7/8" x 3-1/4" x 4' Front rail
(3) 1" x 2-1/2" x 8' Seat slats
(1) 7/8" x 3" x 9' Back slats

HARDWARE & SUPPLIES

Quick-drying epoxy resin
(10) 2" brass panhead screws
Sandpaper
1/2" rope or nylon cord

Recommended Material and Finish: red oak and polyurethane

CONSTRUCTION PROCEDURE

(see Assembly Diagram, Arm Detail, and Side View)

1. Before starting on the swing, transfer the arm pattern from the Arm Detail illustration, and the seat rail pattern from the Side View illustration, to pieces of poster board or thin plywood. (Note that the full length of each seat rail is 17". Instructions for cutting the rails' tenons are given at a later point.)

2. Use a jigsaw or band saw to cut out the plywood patterns; use a utility knife if the patterns are on poster board.

3. Size the upright and seat-back rail stock by ripping two 2-5/8" pieces from the 5-1/2" board.

4. From each of these 11' boards, cut a 13-1/2" front upright, a 21" rear upright, a 46-1/4" seat back rail, a 22" arm blank, and a 17" seat rail.

5. Cut a 46-1/4" front rail from the 4' piece of 3-1/4" stock.

6. Next, cut five 48" seat slats from the 1" x 2-1/2" stock.

7. Cut the 7/8" x 3" stock into seven 14" back slats.

8. Cut 1/2" x 1" x 2" tenons on the back slats' ends.

9. Transfer the arm pattern to the two 22" arm blanks.

10. Lay out and cut a 1/2" x 1" x 2" tenon and a 1/2" x 1" x 2" mortise on each arm, using the Arm Detail as a placement guide.

11. Then use a jigsaw or band saw to cut around the curved lines.

12. Transfer the seat rail pattern to the two 17" seat rail blanks.

13. Cut two 1/2" x 1" x 2" tenons on each rail, and then cut along the exterior lines.

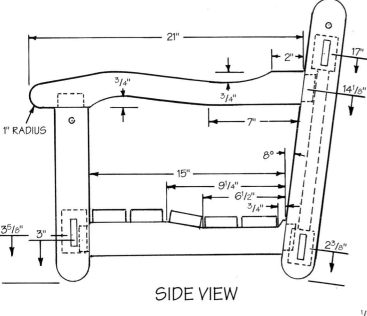

SIDE VIEW

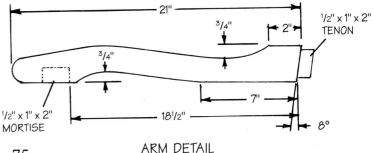

ARM DETAIL

ASSEMBLY DIAGRAM

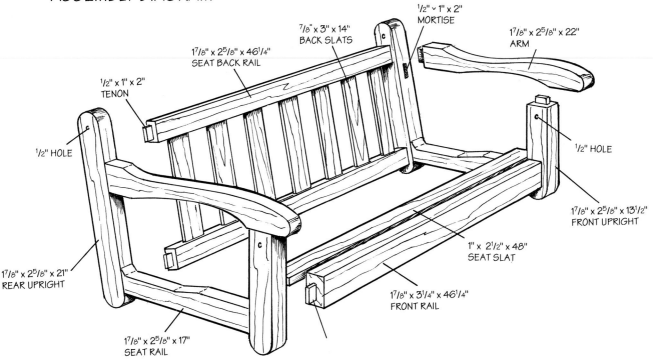

14. Locate the three 46-1/4" rails, and cut a 1/2" x 1" x 2" tenon on each end of all three.

15. Next, cut a 1/2" x 1" x 2" tenon on the top of each 13-1/2" front upright.

16. On the inner face of each front upright, lay out and cut a 1/2" x 1" x 2" mortise, centered 3-5/8" from the bottom.

17. On the adjacent, inner edge of each upright, lay out and cut a 1/2" x 1" x 2" mortise, centered 3" up from the bottom.

18. Lay out and cut a similar mortise at the same location on each of the rear uprights, but angle this mortise up slightly (8°) to compensate for the slant of the swing's back.

19. Cut an identical angled mortise along the same edge of each rear upright, centered 14-1/8" up from the bottom.

20. On the inner faces of each rear upright, lay out and cut two 1/2" x 1" x 2" mortises, one centered 2-3/8" from the bottom and the other 17" from the bottom.

21. To provide points of attachment for the rope, bore a 1/2" hole, 2" from the top, through each of the four uprights.

22. Complete the uprights by cutting a 1-5/16" radius half-circle on their bottoms and on the top of each rear upright.

23. Locate the two 2-5/8" x 46-1/4" seat back rails, and clamp them together face-to-face.

24. At the center of each rail, lay out a 1/2" x 1" x 2" mortise.

25. Then lay out three more mortises to each side, on 6" centers.

26. Remove the clamps, and cut the fourteen mortises.

27. Dry fit all components, and make adjustments as necessary.

28. Use epoxy resin to assemble the two side frames.

29. While the frames are drying, glue the back-rest assembly, making sure that the components are square.

30. Join the two frame halves with the front rail and back-rest assembly, using epoxy at the joints.

31. Glue and screw each of the five seat slats across the side rails, maintaining an equal spacing of about 3/8".

32. Sand the finished swing, and apply two coats of polyurethane.

33. When the protective coating has dried, attach the ropes. There are many ways to do this, but one fail-safe method is to insert the ropes from the outside of each upright, tying a knot to keep them from pulling back through the holes.

76

SWING

On autumn days, breathtaking views of turning leaves are all the more spectacular from a garden swing. And in the summer, when nature's oven seems to be on permanent broil instead of gentle simmer, and when the air is as still and heavy as a wool blanket, creating your own cool breeze is as simple as climbing into the swing and setting it in motion. You can enjoy your swing in hundreds of ways, of course, though once your friends and family have discovered its charms, you may not get to use it as often as you'd like!

TREE
SURROUND

SUGGESTED TOOLS

Circular saw
Hand saw
Framing square
Hammer
Mallet
Chisel
3/8" electric drill
Table saw with dado blade (optional)

MATERIALS LIST

(3) 2 x 4 x 12' Rear and front legs
(2) 2 x 4 x 12' Seat rails
(2) 1 x 6 x 12' Seat slats
(3) 1 x 6 x 8' Skirt boards and seat-back slats
(1) 1 x 6 x 8' Seat-back rails
(1) 1 x 4 x 4' Filler strips and caps

HARDWARE & SUPPLIES

Quick-drying epoxy resin
8d finishing nails
(6) 3/8" x 3-1/2" galvanized bolts with washers and nuts
(48) No. 6 x 1-1/4" deck screws
Sandpaper

Recommended Material and Finish:
red oak and polyurethane

TOP VIEW

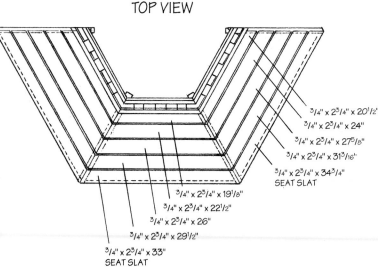

3/4" x 2³/4" x 20¹/2"
3/4" x 2³/4" x 24"
3/4" x 2³/4" x 27⁵/8"
3/4" x 2³/4" x 31³/16"
3/4" x 2³/4" x 34³/4"
SEAT SLAT

3/4" x 2³/4" x 19¹/8"
3/4" x 2³/4" x 22¹/2"
3/4" x 2³/4" x 26"
3/4" x 2³/4" x 29¹/2"
3/4" x 2³/4" x 33"
SEAT SLAT

Each half of the surround consists of three sections—one center section, and two side sections.

LEGS
(see Assembly Diagram)

1. Cut two of the five 12' 2 x 4s into eight rear-leg blanks. Be sure that each blank is equal in length—approximately 36".

2. Lay out and cut a slope on each of the blanks, starting at a point 16-1/4" from the bottom of each leg and tapering to a width of 1" at the top (see Assembly Diagram).

3. Cut eight 16-1/4" front legs from one of the other 12' 2 x 4s.

4. On each of the sixteen front and rear legs, cut two 1/2"-wide x 1-1/2" x 2-1/2" mortises, centered 3-3/4" and 14-1/2" up from the bottom.

SEAT RAILS
(see Assembly Diagram)

5. Cut sixteen upper and lower 16-1/2" seat rails from the other two 12' 2 x 4s.

6. On both ends of each rail, cut a 1/2" x 1-1/2" x 2-1/2" tenon.

7. Dry fit the legs and rails, making adjustments as necessary. Then disassemble them.

8. Cut a double 30° bevel on the front edge of each front leg. Cut a similar bevel along the upper, sloped edges of each rear leg, stopping at the finished seat height of 17".

9. Glue the legs and rails together with epoxy resin, and clamp them together until the epoxy has dried.

SEAT SLATS
(see Assembly Diagram and Top View)

10. Rip the three 12' and four 8' 1 x 6s into fourteen 3/4" x 2-3/4" pieces of stock.

11. Lay out five pairs of angled center slats—five for each center section—on two of the 12' pieces of stock. Each slat has a 30° angle at its end, so you can mini-

78

ASSEMBLY DIAGRAM

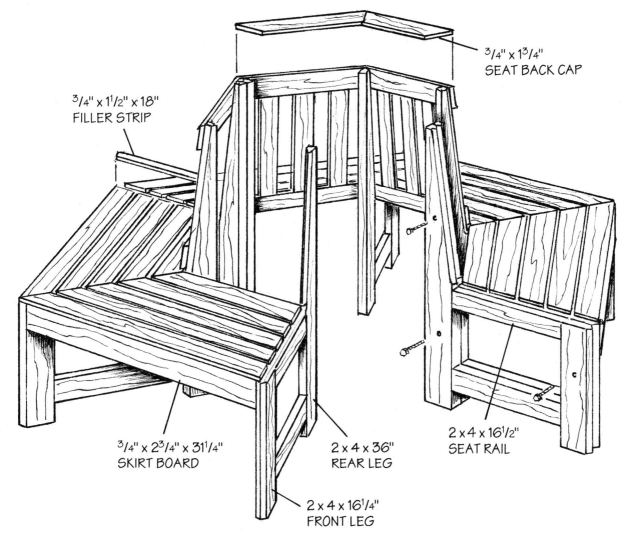

³/4" x 1³/4"
SEAT BACK CAP

³/4" x 1¹/2" x 18"
FILLER STRIP

³/4" x 2³/4" x 31¹/4"
SKIRT BOARD

2 x 4 x 36"
REAR LEG

2 x 4 x 16¹/2"
SEAT RAIL

2 x 4 x 16¹/4"
FRONT LEG

mize lumber use by laying out the slats with their angled ends facing each other. Measured along their long ends, the slats' lengths should be 19-1/8", 22-1/2", 26", 29-1/2", and 33" long. Cut the slats out.

12. Use finishing nails to attach one of the longest and one of the shortest slats to two leg-and-rail assemblies, lapping the slats to the center of the upper seat rails.

13. As you attach the other three slats, use a straightedge, aligned along the ends of the two nailed slats, as a placement guide.

14. Form another center section by repeating this process with the other five slats and another pair of leg-and-rail assemblies.

15. From the other four 12' pieces of ripped stock, lay out and cut twenty similarly angled slats—four of each size. Slats in each set of four should measure 20-1/2", 24", 27-5/8", 31-3/16", and 34-3/4" along their longest sides.

16. Use two slats of each size to join two more leg-and-rail assemblies to both sides of each center section. Again, extend the slats only to the center of the upper seat rails; use a straightedge as a stop.

SKIRT BOARDS
(see Assembly Diagram and Side View)

17. Cut four 33" and two 31-1/4" skirt boards (measured on their long faces)—each with 30° miters at both ends—from two of the 8' sections of ripped stock. Be sure to lay these out with their mitered ends facing each other, or you'll run out of stock.

18. Use finishing nails to attach the 31-1/4" skirt boards between the front legs of the two center sections; their long faces should rest flush with the inner edge of the front leg bevels.

19. Attach the 33" skirt boards between the front legs in adjacent sections.

79

TREE
SURROUND

Assembling garden furniture on site can be a frustrating experience, so we've designed this stately tree surround in two sections, which can be separated with as little effort as they're put together. Do check your selected location before you start to build, however! Dips and ridges in the earth aren't insurmountable problems. A shovel and a little elbow grease will level an area for the surround's legs, but beware if you find roots emerging around the tree's base. These aren't removable and may interfere with the surround's stability once it's in place.

ASSEMBLY OF BENCH SECTIONS
(see Assembly Diagram)

20. Clamp the two bench halves together after checking to see that the outer legs on each half are correctly aligned.

21. Through each of the two sets of paired rear legs, along their faces' center lines, drill two 3/8" pilot holes, one 8" up from the bottom and the other 12" down from the top.

22. Through each set of paired front legs, drill a similar hole 8" up from the bottom.

23. Insert and tighten 3/8" bolts (with washers and nuts) through the six holes.

SEAT-BACK SLATS AND RAILS
(see Side View and Assembly Diagram)

24. Once the bench has been secured, cut twenty-four 15-1/2" seat-back slats from four of the remaining 2-3/4" sections.

25. On both ends of each slat, cut a 1/4" x 1"-long x 1-1/2" tenon.

26. From one of the other two 8' sections, cut two pairs of upper and lower seat-back rails for the center sections. Each rail should be laid out and cut with a 30° compound miter—angled at 3-1/2°—at each end. The longest measurement of two rails should be 15", and the longest measurement of the other two should be 16-7/8".

27. Using screws (but not epoxy), attach one upper seat-back rail flush with the top of each center section.

28. Attach the lower rails (also with screws) 13-1/2" below the upper rails.

29. From the last 8' piece of ripped stock, cut four more pairs of upper and lower rails. Each rail should have a similar compound miter on it; lengths for each pair should be 16-1/2"and 18-3/8" respectively.

30. With screws, attach these pairs to the rear legs of the remaining four sections, maintaining a 13-1/2" spacing on each assembly.

31. Using a framing square and a tape measure, establish the center line of each seat back.

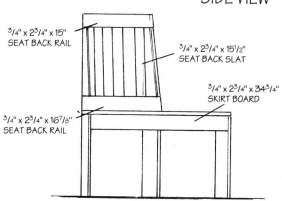

3/4" x 2 3/4" x 15"
SEAT BACK RAIL

3/4" x 2 3/4" x 15 1/2"
SEAT BACK SLAT

3/4" x 2 3/4" x 34 3/4"
SKIRT BOARD

3/4" x 2 3/4" x 16 7/8"
SEAT BACK RAIL

32. Using these center lines as guides, place and equally space four back slats in each assembly, and mark the location of their tenons on the rails' faces.

33. Remove the seat-back slats and the rails.

34. Using a drill and chisel, cut the forty-eight 1/4" x 1" x 1-1/2" mortises in the rails.

35. After the mortises have been checked for fit, reattach the rail pairs with the seat-back slats in place.

FILLER STRIPS AND CAPS
(see Assembly Diagram)

36. To make the two filler strips, cut an 18" piece from the 1 x 4 stock, and rip two 1-1/2" strips from it.

37. Cut a pair of 30° angles at each end so that the boards measure 18" long at their longest points.

38. Lay the filler strips in the voids at the seat joints, and attach them with finishing nails. (Be careful to drive nails into only one of the two seat rails at each joint, or you won't be able to disassemble your tree surround when you need to!)

39. Rip the remaining 1 x 4 material in half to form the seat-back cap.

40. Cut a 30° starting miter on one of the boards.

41. Position the mitered board flush with the front edge of the upper seat-back rail.

42. Mark and then cut the board to length.

43. Repeat this process around the perimeter of the bench.

44. Finish the project by sanding and applying two or three coats of clear sealer.

MAKING YOUR GARDEN GROW

By early spring, winter-bound gardeners are close to insanity. The urge to inhale the sweet smells of newly mown grass and to plunge hands into freshly turned loam is almost uncontrollable. But nothing dampens this glorious madness as quickly as scrounging through a basement in search of musty clay pots. Or traipsing back and forth from a new planting bed to the concrete drive where you've set out your tools. Or discovering that you've run out of space for all those purchased plants.

Hang on to your lunacy! A potting table provides a single, organized storage and work space. A boot bench makes a comfy home for mud-laden shoes, tools, and other garden gadgetry. Planters— whether you place them on a patio or right in the middle of a sunny yard— guarantee those extra square feet of planting space that you've always craved. And a modular grouping of planters— with benches included—are perfect spots from which to scan your day's labor. Every one of these projects will help you extend your enthusiasm and energy through the gardening season.

RECTANGULAR
PLANTER

SUGGESTED TOOLS

Circular saw
Hammer
Chisel
3/8" electric drill
Screwdriver
Table saw
Router (optional)

MATERIALS LIST

(1) 1 x 8 x 14' Rails, posts, and caps
(1) 1 x 2 x 8' End and side supports
(1) 1/4" x 4' x 4' ext. plywood Panels

HARDWARE & SUPPLIES

Quick-drying epoxy resin
No. 6 x 1-1/4" deck screws
6d finishing nails
Sandpaper
8d common nails

Recommended Material and Finish:
redwood and water sealer

CONSTRUCTION PROCEDURE
(see Assembly Diagram and End Section)

1. Cut a 9' section from the 14' 1 x 8.

2. Rip two 2-3/8" boards from this section. Rip an additional 2" strip for later use as end and side caps.

3. Cut two 28-1/4" side rails and two 6" end rails from each of the 2-3/8" boards.

4. At both ends of each rail, cut a 1/4" x 1"-long x 1-7/8" tenon.

5. Rip two 2-5/8"-wide boards from the remaining 1 x 8 material, and cut a 45° bevel along one side of each.

6. Cut four 13-1/2" corner posts from each of these beveled boards.

7. Along the non-beveled edge of each post, cut two 1/4" x 1-7/8" x 1"-deep mortises, 1/4" in from each end.

8. Set the table saw or router to cut a 1/4"-wide x 1/4"-deep groove along one edge of each rail, 1/4" from the back (or inner) face, and complete these cuts.

9. Cut grooves of the same dimensions between the mortises on each post, 1/4" in from the posts' narrow faces.

10. Dry fit the posts and rails, and make adjustments as necessary.

11. From the 1/4" plywood, cut two 9-1/8" x 26-5/8" panels and two 9-1/8" x 4-3/8" panels.

12. Reassemble the individual post-and-rail frames with the plywood panels in place, applying epoxy resin to the mortise and tenon joints and squaring the frames as you work. Allow the panels to float within their frames.

13. While the epoxy is drying, rip 3/4" x 3/4" strips from the 1 x 2 stock.

14. From the ripped stock, cut four 30" side supports and four 7-3/4" end supports, squared at both ends.

15. Drill two 1/8" holes along the center line of each support, 3/8" in from each end.

16. Rest the long side-panel assemblies face down on a flat work surface, and position the four 30" supports 7/8" in from their top and bottom edges. The ends of

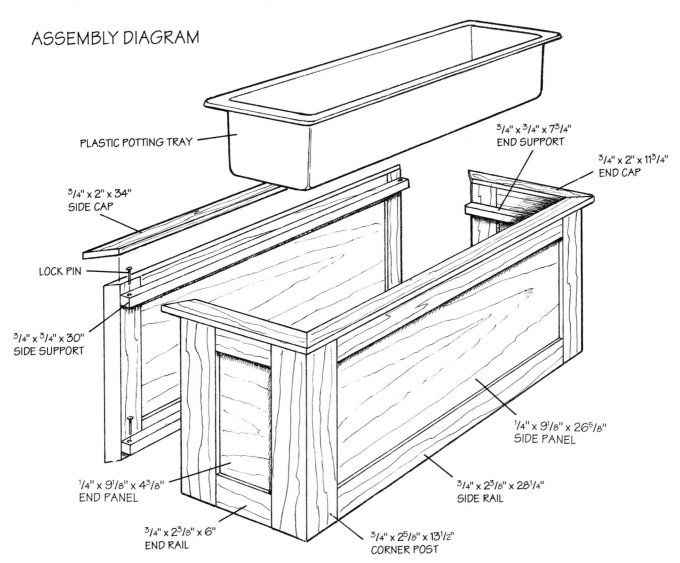

PLASTIC POTTING TRAY

3/4" x 3/4" x 7³/4"
END SUPPORT

3/4" x 2" x 11³/4"
END CAP

3/4" x 2" x 34"
SIDE CAP

LOCK PIN

3/4" x 3/4" x 30"
SIDE SUPPORT

1/4" x 9¹/8" x 26⁵/8"
SIDE PANEL

1/4" x 9¹/8" x 4³/8"
END PANEL

3/4" x 2³/8" x 28¹/4"
SIDE RAIL

3/4" x 2³/8" x 6"
END RAIL

3/4" x 2⁵/8" x 13¹/2"
CORNER POST

each support should be flush with the posts' bevels, and their holes should run parallel to the panels (see Assembly Diagram for correct placement).

17. Fasten the supports in place with epoxy and 1-1/4" deck screws.

18. Repeat this process with the end-panel assemblies, fastening their 7-1/4" supports 1-5/8" from the top and bottom edges.

19. From the material left from step 2, cut two 34" and two 11-3/4" caps.

20. Cut a 45° miter on both ends of all caps, so that their short edges measure 30" and 7-3/4" respectively.

21. Glue and nail the caps so that these short edges are flush with the inside face of each panel; use 6d finishing nails.

22. Sand the panels, and apply two to three coats of clear sealer.

23. To assemble the planter, lap the internal supports, and insert a 1/8" pin in each hole. Pins can be made by cutting off 8d nails.

24. Insert a plastic potting tray. (In the autumn, just remove the tray and pins, and the planter will collapse into four easy-to-store panels.)

END SECTION

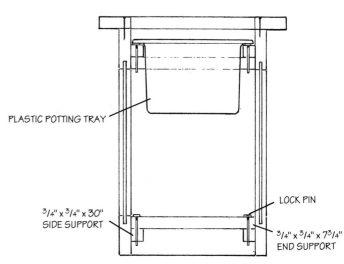

PLASTIC POTTING TRAY

3/4" x 3/4" x 30"
SIDE SUPPORT

LOCK PIN

3/4" x 3/4" x 7³/4"
END SUPPORT

RECTANGULAR PLANTER

We can't tell you that we've discovered the secret to rearranging a garden in mid-bloom, but we can offer you a way to move the prized blossoms in your planter without killing them—or yourself. And you won't need to recruit a muscle-bound neighbor or a landscape gardener to help. Instead, just remove the standard-sized plastic container in this Rectangular Planter, and then disassemble the planter itself. Its knockdown design makes it a restless gardener's dream.

RAISED-PANEL PLANTER
(small)

This sturdy planter isn't as small (or as difficult to build) as you might think. Its interior is spacious enough to accept a variety of containers, and the handsome raised-panel design couldn't be easier to create. Set your table saw at the positions indicated in our instructions, zip each panel edge through twice, then pat yourself on the back. We've attached a shelf 15" up from the bottom of the project, but if you'd like to raise or lower it to suit your plants, by all means do.

RAISED-PANEL PLANTER
(small)

SUGGESTED TOOLS

Circular saw
Hammer
Chisel
Screwdriver
Table saw with dado blade
Router (optional)

MATERIALS LIST

(2) 1 x 12 x 8' Raised panels
(1) 2 x 4 x 8' Rails
(1) 2 x 4 x 10' Uprights and stiles
(1) 1/2" x 2' x 2' ext. plywood Shelf supports
(1) 3/4" x 2' x 2' ext. plywood Planter shelf

HARDWARE & SUPPLIES

Sandpaper
Quick-drying epoxy resin
(24) 1" finishing screws
(32) 6d finishing nails
No. 6 x 1-1/4" deck screws

Recommended Material and Finish:
redwood and water sealer

RAISED PANELS
(see Assembly Diagram and Cutting Sequence)

1. Cut four 20-7/8" panel blanks from each of the 8' 1 x 12s.

2. Set the trim blade on the table saw at an 8° angle off vertical and to a depth of 2-3/4". Adjust the fence so that it is 1/4" from the blade at the table surface.

3. Choose the best sides of the panel blanks, and mark them as the face sides.

4. Pass each panel through the table saw, with its back side riding along the fence. Thirty-two cuts will be required for the eight blanks.

5. Readjust the saw to a vertical position, with the blade riding 1/4" from the fence at a depth of 1/2".

6. Pass all four edges of each blank through the blade at this setting.

7. Sand the panels, and set them aside for later assembly.

UPRIGHTS, STILES, AND RAILS
(see Assembly Diagram)

8. Set the table saw to rip at 1-1/2".

9. Rip two 1-1/2" x 1-1/2" lengths from the 8' 2 x 4 and two 1-1/2" x 1-1/2" lengths from the 10' 2 x 4 by passing each 2 x 4 through the table saw twice.

10. Form the four corner uprights by cutting two 27" lengths from each of the 10' pieces.

11. To create a decorative point on each upright, make a 45° cut on each face, 3/4" down from the top.

12. Cut two 21" stiles from each of the remaining two pieces.

13. Set the dado blade or router bit to cut a 1/4"-wide and 1/2"-deep groove.

14. Cut a groove of these dimensions down the center of two opposing faces of each 21" stile. (Eight cuts are necessary.)

15. Then, using the same blade or bit setting, make cuts 22-1/2" long down the centers of two adjoining faces of each upright. Start these cuts 2-1/4" from the bottom of each upright, and stop them 2-1/4" from the top. Clean out the ends of each cut with a chisel.

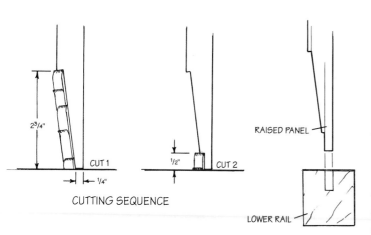

2³/₄"

CUT 1

1/4"

1/2"

CUT 2

RAISED PANEL

LOWER RAIL

CUTTING SEQUENCE

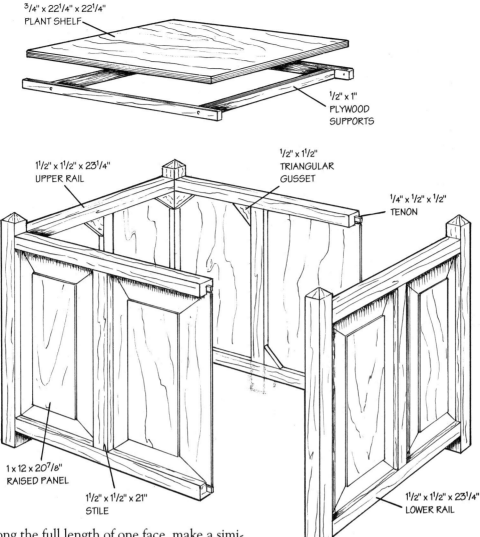

3/4" x 22-1/4" x 22-1/4"
PLANT SHELF

1/2" x 1"
PLYWOOD
SUPPORTS

1-1/2" x 1-1/2" x 23-1/4"
UPPER RAIL

1/2" x 1-1/2"
TRIANGULAR
GUSSET

1/4" x 1/2" x 1/2"
TENON

1 x 12 x 20-7/8"
RAISED PANEL

1-1/2" x 1-1/2" x 21"
STILE

1-1/2" x 1-1/2" x 23-1/4"
LOWER RAIL

1-1/2" x 1-1/2" x 27"
CORNER UPRIGHT

16. Next, along the full length of one face, make a similar cut on each of the two 1-1/2" x 1-1/2" x 8' sections.

17. To make the eight upper and lower side rails, cut four 23-1/4" lengths from each of these 8' sections.

18. Cut a 1/4"-wide x 1/2" x 1/2" tenon, oriented in the same plane as the groove, on the end of each rail and stile.

PLANTER ASSEMBLY
(see Assembly Diagram)

19. Join each of the four pairs of panels with a center stile.

20. Place rails on the top and bottom edges of each raised-panel assembly so that the ends of the tenons are flush with the panels' edges.

21. Dry fit the assemblies to the uprights, making any necessary adjustments.

22. When the fit is satisfactory, use epoxy resin to glue the tenons on the stiles and rails. Fasten them with finishing screws inserted from the inside, squaring the planter as you work. (Allow the panels to float within the frames.)

23. Make the plywood supports by cutting four 1" strips from the 1/2" plywood. The length of these strips will depend on the final, interior dimensions of your assembled planter.

24. Cut sixteen 1-1/2" x 1-1/2" triangular gussets from the remaining 1/2" plywood.

25. When the glued planter has dried, attach the gussets with epoxy and finishing nails.

26. Trim the 1" strips of plywood to fit the interior dimensions of the planter, and use deck screws to attach them 15" up from the planter's base.

27. Cut a 22-1/4" x 22-1/4" plant shelf from the 3/4" plywood.

28. Attach the shelf to the supports with 1-1/4" screws.

29. Sand all surfaces.

30. Apply two coats of water sealer to the assembled planter.

RAISED-PANEL PLANTER
(large)

The unique raised panels that distinguish this planter from any you might pick up at a gardening store are just as easy to make as those of its smaller relative. In fact, the only difference is that there are four more of them in this version. Try filling a planter of each size with fragrant, flowering plants or herbs and placing them on your deck or porch for those days when you'd rather lounge close to home than amble along a garden path.

RAISED-PANEL PLANTER
(large)

SUGGESTED TOOLS

Circular saw
Hammer
Chisel
Screwdriver
Table saw with dado blade
Router (optional)

MATERIALS LIST

(3) 1 x 12 x 8' Raised panels
(1) 2 x 4 x 12' Rails
(1) 2 x 4 x 14' Uprights and stiles
(1) 1/2" x 2' x 4' ext. plywood Shelf
    supports
(1) 3/4" x 2' x 4' ext. plywood Planter
    shelf

HARDWARE & SUPPLIES

Sandpaper
Quick-drying epoxy resin
(36) 1" finishing screws
(48) 6d finishing nails
No. 6 x 1-1/4" deck screws

Recommended Material and Finish:
   redwood and water sealer

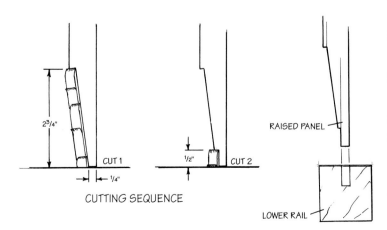

CUTTING SEQUENCE

RAISED PANELS
(see Assembly Diagram and Cutting Sequence)

1. Cut four 20-7/8" panel blanks from each of the 8' 1 x 12s.

2. Set the trim blade on the table saw at an 8° angle off vertical and to a depth of 2-3/4". Adjust the fence so that it is 1/4" from the blade at the table surface.

3. Choose and mark the best (face) sides of the panel blanks.

4. Pass each panel through the table saw with its back side riding along the fence. Forty-eight cuts will be required for the twelve blanks.

5. Readjust the saw to a vertical position, with the blade riding 1/4" from the fence at a depth of 1/2".

6. Pass all four edges of each blank through the blade at this setting.

7. Sand the panels, and set them aside for later assembly.

UPRIGHTS, STILES, AND RAILS
(see Assembly Diagram)

8. Set the table saw to rip at 1-1/2".

9. Pass each of the two 2 x 4s through the table saw twice to yield four 1-1/2" x 1-1/2" pieces of stock.

10. Form the corner and center uprights by cutting three 27" lengths from each of the 14' pieces.

11. To create a decorative point on each upright, make a 45° cut on each face, 3/4" down from the top.

12. Cut three 21" stiles from each of the pieces that remain from the 14' boards, for a total of six stiles.

13. Set the dado blade or router bit to cut a 1/4"-wide x 1/2"-deep groove.

14. Cut a groove of these dimensions down the center of two opposing faces of each stile. (Twelve cuts are necessary.)

15. Then, using the same blade or bit setting, make cuts 22-1/2" long down the center of two adjoining faces of the four corner uprights. Start these cuts 2-1/4" from the bottom of each upright, and stop them 2-1/4" from the top.

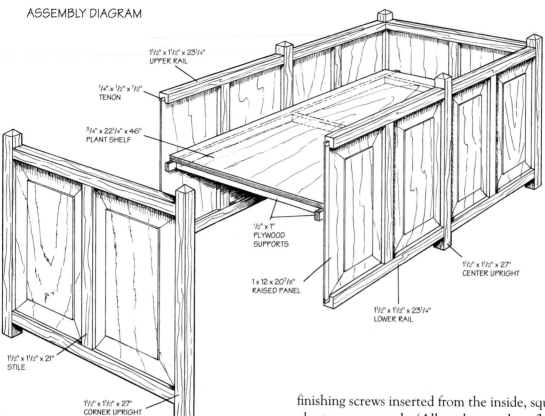

1¹/₂" x 1¹/₂" x 23¹/₄"
UPPER RAIL

¹/₄".x ¹/₂" x ¹/₂"
TENON

³/₄" x 22¹/₄" x 46"
PLANT SHELF

¹/₂" x 1"
PLYWOOD
SUPPORTS

1 x 12 x 20⁷/₈"
RAISED PANEL

1¹/₂" x 1¹/₂" x 27"
CENTER UPRIGHT

1¹/₂" x 1¹/₂" x 23¹/₄"
LOWER RAIL

1¹/₂" x 1¹/₂" x 21"
STILE

1¹/₂" x 1¹/₂" x 27"
CORNER UPRIGHT

16. On the two center uprights, make this same groove on two opposing (rather than adjoining) faces.

17. Next, along the full length of one face, make a similar cut on each of the two 1-1/2" x 1-1/2" x 12' sections.

18. To make the twelve upper and lower side rails, cut six 23-1/4" lengths from each of these 12' sections.

19. Cut a 1/4"-wide x 1/2" x 1/2" tenon, oriented in the same plane as the groove, on the end of each rail and stile.

PLANTER ASSEMBLY
(see Assembly Diagram)

20. Join each of the six pairs of panels with a center stile.

21. Place rails on the top and bottom edges of each raised panel assembly so that the ends of the rail tenons are flush with the panels' edges.

22. Dry fit the assemblies to the uprights, making any necessary adjustments.

23. When the fit is satisfactory, use epoxy resin to glue the tenons on the stiles and rails, and fasten them with

finishing screws inserted from the inside, squaring the planter as you work. (Allow the panels to float within the frames.)

24. Make the plywood supports by cutting five 1"-wide strips from the 1/2" plywood. Four strips should be at least 4' in length, and the remaining strip should be at least 2' long. These will be trimmed to the interior dimensions of the planter.

25. Cut twenty-four 1-1/2" x 1-1/2" triangular gussets from the remaining 1/2" plywood.

26. When the glued planter has dried, attach the gussets (two to each panel) with epoxy and 1" finishing nails. (Though these aren't portrayed in the assembly diagram, they should be fit into the corners formed by the rails, stiles, and uprights. Refer to the smaller Raised-Panel Planter Assembly Diagram for correct placement.)

27. Trim the 1" strips of plywood to fit the interior of the planter, and use deck screws to attach them 15" up from the planter's base.

28. Cut a 22-1/4" x 46" plant shelf from the 3/4" plywood.

29. Attach the shelf to the supports with 1-1/4" deck screws.

30. Sand all surfaces, and apply two coats of water sealer to the assembled planter.

CHIPPENDALE-PANEL PLANTER (small)

SUGGESTED TOOLS

Circular saw
Hammer
Chisel
3/8" electric drill
Screwdriver
Jigsaw
Router
Table saw with dado blade (optional)

MATERIALS LIST

(1) 1/2" x 23" x 25-1/4" plywood Jig
(1) 1/4" x 4' x 4 ' ext. plywood Panels and jig strips
(1) 2 x 4 x 10' Lattice slats
(2) 2 x 4 x 8' Uprights and rails
(1) 3/4" x 2' x 2' ext. plywood Plant shelf
(1) 1/2" x 2' x 2' ext. plywood Gussets and support strips

HARDWARE & SUPPLIES

Quick-drying epoxy resin
(16) 1" finishing screws
6d finishing nails
No. 6 x 1-1/4" deck screws
Sandpaper

Recommended Material and Finish:
redwood and water sealer

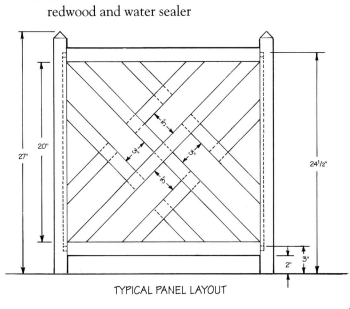

TYPICAL PANEL LAYOUT

PANELS
(see Typical Panel Layout)

1. Cut a jig 23" long x 25-1/4" wide from a piece of scrap 1/2" plywood.

2. Cut and then glue four 1/4" x 1" plywood strips around the outer edges of the jig's face, with their 1" widths facing down. The visible surface of the plywood will now be 21" x 23-1/4", and the strips will provide a 1/4" deep lip around the interior section.

3. With a jigsaw, cut a 20" x 22-1/4" center opening in the plywood, leaving a 1/2" band between the edges of the opening and the interior edges of the strips.

4. Cut four panels, each 21" x 23-1/4", from the remaining 1/4" plywood stock.

5. Place one panel into the jig; it should fit neatly between (and flush with the top of) the surrounding strips.

6. Flip the jig and panel upside-down, and rest them on a flat surface.

7. Next, rip the 10' piece of 2 x 4 stock into several 1/2" x 1-1/2" strips.

8. From these strips, cut
(a) eight pieces 28-1/4" measured from long point to short point on parallel 45° cuts;
(b) eight pieces 11-3/16" long, measured from the squared end to the long end of a 45° cut;
(c) eight pieces 9-9/16" long, measured from the squared end to the long end of a 45° cut;
(d) eight pieces 6-11/16" long, measured from the squared end to the long end of a 45° cut;
(e) eight pieces 5-1/16" long, measured from the squared end to the long end of a 45° cut.

9. Starting with two 28-1/4" lattice slats, lay two pieces of each size onto the panel backing, which should be exposed through the back of the jig. Use the illustration as a placement guide.

10. Cut half-lap joints at each intersection.

11. Dry fit all joints, and make adjustments as necessary. The lattice slats should fit neatly into the cut-out section of the jig.

12. Apply epoxy resin to all half-lap joints and to the back sides of each slat. Glue them in place onto the panel.

13. When the epoxy has dried, remove the panel from the jig, and repeat steps 9 through 12 to assemble each of the other three panels.

14. Set the panels aside for future assembly.

PLANTER CONSTRUCTION
(see Assembly Diagram)

15. Set the table saw to rip at 1-1/2". Pass each of the two 8' 2 x 4s through the saw to yield four 1-1/2" x 1-1/2" x 8' pieces of stock.

16. Form the corner uprights by cutting two of the sections into four 27" lengths. (To create a decorative point on each upright, make a 45° cut on each face, 3/4" down from the top.)

17. Next, set the router (or table saw blade) to cut a 1/4"-wide x 1/2"-deep groove.

18. Make cuts down the centers of two adjoining sides of each upright. These grooves should be 22-1/2" long and should run from a point 2-1/4" from the top to 2-1/4" from the bottom of each upright.

19. On each of the two remaining 8' sections, make a similar cut along the full length of one face.

20. Then cut four 23-1/4" lengths from each of these 8' sections to make the eight upper and lower side rails.

21. On the end of each rail, cut a 1/4"-wide x 1/2" x 1/2" tenon, oriented in the same plane as the groove.

22. Place side rails on the top and bottom edges of each panel so that the ends of the rail tenons are even with the panels' edges.

23. Dry fit the assemblies to the uprights, and make any necessary adjustments.

24. When the fit is satisfactory, glue the tenons to the uprights, and fasten them from the inside with finishing screws, squaring the planter as you work.

25. Cut four 1"-wide supports from the 1/2" x 2' x 2' plywood. These will be trimmed to fit the interior dimensions of the planter.

26. Cut the remaining 1/2" plywood into sixteen 1-1/2" x 1-1/2" triangular gussets.

27. Attach these gussets with epoxy and finishing nails (see Assembly Diagram for placement).

28. Once the glued planter assembly has dried, trim the support strips to size, and screw them to the inside of the planter to create a support 15" up from the planter's base.

29. Cut a 22-1/4" x 22-1/4" plant shelf from the 3/4" plywood.

30. Attach the shelf to the supports with 1-1/4" deck screws.

31. Sand all surfaces.

32. Finish the planter with two coats of water sealer.

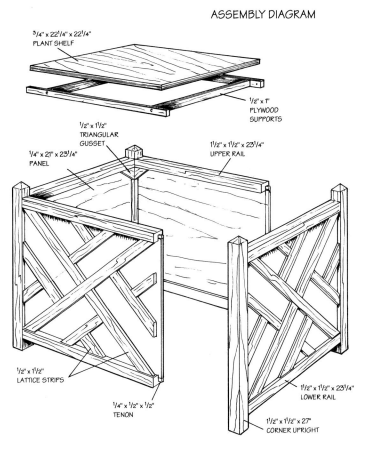

ASSEMBLY DIAGRAM

³/4" x 22¹/4" x 22¹/4"
PLANT SHELF

¹/2" x 1"
PLYWOOD
SUPPORTS

¹/2" x 1¹/2"
TRIANGULAR
GUSSET

¹/4" x 21" x 23¹/4"
PANEL

1¹/2" x 1¹/2" x 23¹/4"
UPPER RAIL

¹/2" x 1¹/2"
LATTICE STRIPS

¹/4" x ¹/2" x ¹/2"
TENON

1¹/2" x 1¹/2" x 23¹/4"
LOWER RAIL

1¹/2" x 1¹/2" x 27"
CORNER UPRIGHT

94

CHIPPENDALE-PANEL PLANTER (small)

Let's face it; many planters sold today are often either poorly disguised dirt-buckets or garish garden props. Fortunately, a planter can be what it should be: functional but attractive, appealing but not so overwhelming in design that it dwarfs its own contents. When you'd love to bring your blooms closer to home, this Chippendale-Panel Planter offers a practical and aesthetically pleasing alternative to anything you might buy. The natural warmth of its redwood, the engaging but subdued panel pattern, and the planter's moderate size will blend well with almost any setting.

CHIPPENDALE-PANEL
PLANTER (large)

SUGGESTED TOOLS

Circular saw
Hammer
Chisel
3/8" electric drill
Jigsaw
Screw driver
Router
Table saw with dado blade (optional)

MATERIALS LIST

(1) 1/2" x 23" x 25-1/4" plywood Jig
(1) 1/4" x 4' x 6 ' ext. plywood Panels
  and jig strips
(2) 2 x 4 x 8' Lattice slats
(3) 2 x 4 x 8' Uprights and rails
(1) 3/4" x 2' x 4' ext. plywood Plant shelf
(1) 1/2" x 2' x 4' ext. plywood Gussets
  and support strips

HARDWARE & SUPPLIES

Quick-drying epoxy resin
(24) 1" finishing screws
6d finishing nails
No. 6 x 1-1/4" deck screws
Sandpaper

Recommended Material and Finish:
  redwood and water sealer

PANELS
(see Typical Panel Layout)

1. Cut a jig 23" long x 25-1/4" wide from a piece of scrap 1/2" plywood.

2. Cut four 1/4" x 1" plywood strips from the short side of the 1/4" plywood, and glue them around the outer edges of the jig's face, with their 1" widths facing down. The visible surface of the plywood will now be 21" x 23-1/4", and the strips will provide a 1/4" retaining lip around the interior section.

3. With a jigsaw, cut a 20" x 22-1/4" center opening in the jig, leaving a 1/2" band between the edges of the opening and the interior edges of the strips.

4. From the remaining 1/4" plywood stock, cut six 21" x 23-1/4" rectangles.

5. Place one of these panels into the jig; it should fit neatly between (and flush with the top of) the surrounding strips.

6. Flip the jig and panel upside-down, and rest them on a flat surface.

7. Next, rip two of the 8' pieces of 2 x 4 stock into 1/2" x 1-1/2" strips by running them through the table saw several times.

8. From these 1/2" x 1-1/2" strips, form the lattice by cutting: (a) twelve pieces 28-1/4" long, measured long point to short point on the parallel 45° cuts;
(b) twelve pieces 11-3/16" long, measured from the squared end to the long end of a 45° cut;
(c) twelve pieces 9-9/16" long, measured from the squared end to the long end of a 45° cut;
(d) twelve pieces 6-11/16" long, measured from the squared end to the long end of a 45° cut;
(e) twelve pieces 5-1/16" long, measured from the squared end to the long end of a 45° cut.

9. Starting with two 28-1/4" lattice slats, lay two pieces of each size onto the panel, which should be exposed through the jig opening. Use the illustration as a placement guide.

10. Cut half-lap joints at each intersection.

11. Dry fit all joints, and make adjustments as necessary. The lattice slats should fit neatly into the jig.

CHIPPENDALE-PANEL PLANTER (large)

Once again, you'll notice that the design elements in many of these projects are attractively coordinated— and sometimes even interchangeable. The lattice pattern on this planter is exactly the same as the pattern on the smaller Chippendale planter, and it's very similar to those on the Chippendale chair and bench too. Arrange a stylish grouping of all four pieces on the patio or in the yard, or highlight a single planter in a garden spot that's special to you.

12. Apply epoxy resin to all half-lap joints and to the back sides of each slat. Then place the slats in position on the panel.

13. When the epoxy has dried, remove the panel from the jig, and repeat steps 9 through 12 to construct the other five panels.

14. Set the panels aside for future assembly.

PLANTER CONSTRUCTION
(see Assembly Diagram)

15. Set the table saw to rip at 1-1/2". Cut six 1-1/2" x 1-1/2" x 8' pieces of stock by passing each of the remaining three 8' 2 x 4s through the table saw twice.

16. Cut six 27" lengths from three of the six pieces to form the corner and center uprights. (To create a decorative point on each upright, make a 45° cut on each face, 3/4" down from the top.)

17. Set the router bit (or dado blade) to cut a 1/4"-wide x 1/2"-deep groove.

18. Make cuts down the centers of two adjoining sides of each of the four corner uprights. These grooves should be 22-1/2" long and should run from a point 2-1/4" from the top to 2-1/4" from the bottom of each upright.

19. On the two center uprights, make this same cut on two opposing (rather than adjoining) faces.

20. On the remaining 8' sections, make a similar cut along the full length of each face.

21. Cut four 23-1/4" lengths from each 8' section to create the twelve upper and lower side rails.

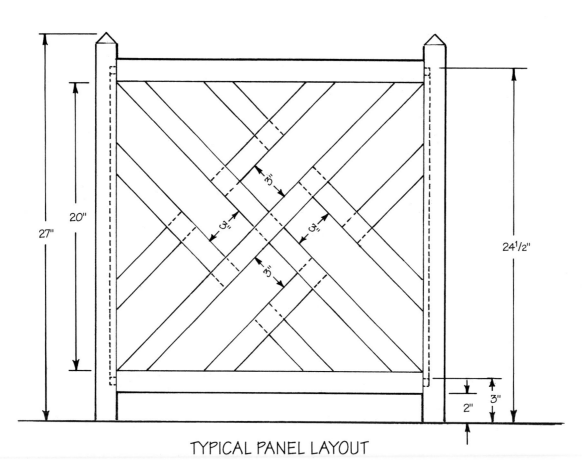

TYPICAL PANEL LAYOUT

98

ASSEMBLY DIAGRAM

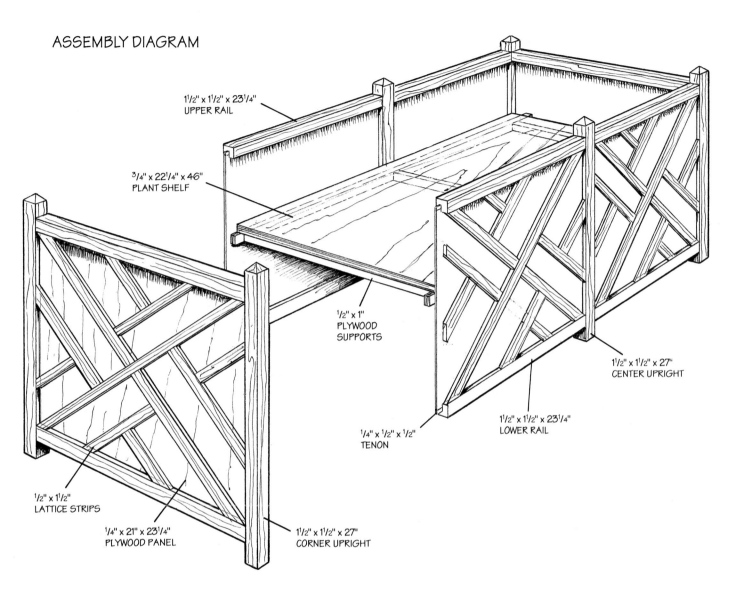

1¹/₂" x 1¹/₂" x 23¹/₄"
UPPER RAIL

³/₄" x 22¹/₄" x 46"
PLANT SHELF

¹/₂" x 1"
PLYWOOD
SUPPORTS

1¹/₂" x 1¹/₂" x 27"
CENTER UPRIGHT

¹/₄" x ¹/₂" x ¹/₂"
TENON

1¹/₂" x 1¹/₂" x 23¹/₄"
LOWER RAIL

¹/₂" x 1¹/₂"
LATTICE STRIPS

¹/₄" x 21" x 23¹/₄"
PLYWOOD PANEL

1¹/₂" x 1¹/₂" x 27"
CORNER UPRIGHT

22. On the ends of each rail, cut a 1/4"-wide x 1/2" x 1/2" tenon, oriented in the same plane as the groove.

23. Place side rails on the top and bottom edges of each lattice panel so that the ends of the rail tenons are even with the plywood edges.

24. Dry fit the assemblies to the uprights, and make any necessary adjustments.

25. When the fit is satisfactory, glue the tenons to the uprights, and fasten them from the inside with finishing screws, squaring the planter as you work.

26. Cut five 1" support strips from the 1/2" plywood. These will be trimmed to the interior dimensions of the planter.

27. Cut twenty-four 1-1/2" triangular gussets from the rest of the 1/2" plywood, and attach them to the planter with epoxy and finishing nails (see the Assembly Diagram for the small Chippendale Planter).

28. Once the glued planter assembly has dried, trim the support strips to size, and screw them to the inside (and across the center) of the planter to create a support 15" up from the planter's base.

29. Cut a 22-1/4" x 46" shelf from the 3/4" plywood.

30. Rest the shelf inside the planter, and attach it to the support strips with 1-1/4" deck screws.

31. Sand all surfaces.

32. Finish the planter with two coats of water sealer.

MODULAR PLANTER AND BENCH ENSEMBLE

Though it's a shame, it's sometimes impossible to sit where you'd like to sit—right in the middle of a flower bed. Though you'd love to surround yourself with soothing scents and colorful blooms, you can't imagine squeezing a garden bench between the azaleas. Fortunately, there is an alternative—bring the plants to your bench instead. This Modular Ensemble—two duckboard benchtops that bridge three handsome planters—permits you to grow your favorite plants within arms' reach. And if the prospect of building a grouping this large seems overwhelming, start with one bench and two planters instead. You can always add to the basic ensemble once you're feeling more confident.

MODULAR PLANTER
AND BENCH ENSEMBLE

SUGGESTED TOOLS

Circular saw
Hack saw
3/8" electric drill
Screwdriver
Table saw with dado blade (optional)

MATERIALS LIST

(1) 1 x 4 x 10' Spacers, template, and supports
(11) 1 x 4 x 6' Seat slats
(1) 3/8" x 36" All-thread tension rod

HARDWARE & SUPPLIES

Sandpaper
(4) 3/8" nuts with washers
(8) 1" finishing screws
(8) No. 10 x 2-1/2" deck screws

Recommended Material and Finish:
redwood and water sealer

DUCKBOARD PLANTER BENCH

SPACERS, LOWER SUPPORTS, AND SLATS

(see Assembly Diagram)

1. Cut twenty 1 x 4 x 3-1/2" spacers from the 10' 1 x 4.

2. From the remaining material, cut a 7" long template. Then drill a 3/8" pilot hole in it, centered 1-3/4" in from either end.

3. Also cut two 14-1/2" lengths from the remaining material.

4. Form the four lower supports by first ripping each of these 14-1/2" lengths down the center and then cutting 45° bevels on their ends.

5. In each short edge of the lower supports, drill two 3/8" holes; the holes should be approximately 3/8" deep, and should be positioned 4" in from each end. Finish drilling through the width of the boards with a 1/8" bit.

6. Drill a countersink hole—large enough to accept a 3/8" nut and washer—in the center of four of the twenty spacers.

7. Next, check the lengths of all eleven 6' 1 x 4s (the seat slats), and trim if necessary.

8. Rest the template flush with the end of one of the seat slats; the center of the pilot hole should be 5-1/4" in from the end of the slat.

9. Using the pilot hole as a guide, drill a 3/8" hole through each end of the slat. Repeat this process to make holes in nine of the eleven seat slats.

10. Using the same template, drill holes directly through the center of all twenty spacers, including the four countersunk spacers.

11. Sand and seal all components, and set them aside for future assembly.

12. Use a hack saw to cut two 14-1/4" tension rods from the 3/8" all-thread rod. (Cutting the waste from the center of the rod will assure that one end of each 14-1/4" length is free of burrs.)

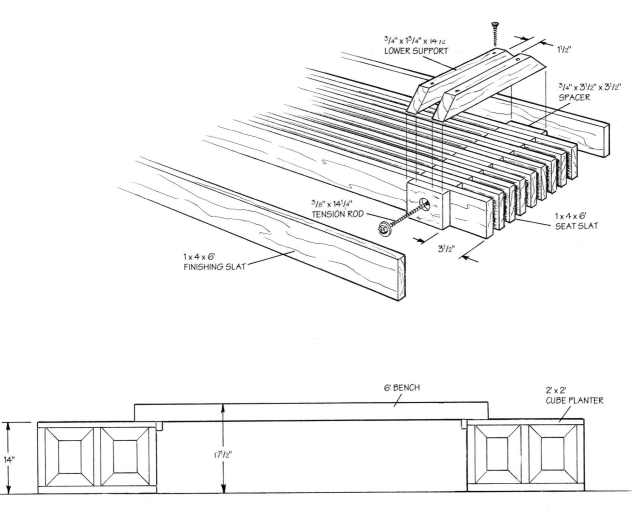

3/4" x 1³/4" x 14¹/2"
LOWER SUPPORT

1¹/2"

3/4" x 3¹/2" x 3¹/2"
SPACER

3/8" x 14¹/4"
TENSION ROD

1 x 4 x 6'
SEAT SLAT

3¹/2"

1 x 4 x 6'
FINISHING SLAT

6' BENCH

2' x 2'
CUBE PLANTER

14"

17¹/2"

ASSEMBLY

(see Assembly Diagram)

13. Thread a nut onto and flush with the cut end of each rod. Then slip a washer over the rod's opposite end so that it rests against the back of the nut.

14. Start stacking the slats and spacers onto the rods. Begin with two of the four countersunk spacers, one on each rod. Slide these on countersink-first.

15. Follow the countersunk spacers with a bench slat, and continue to alternate slats and spacers until nine slats have been added. Add the last two countersunk spacers.

16. Check the alignment of all the spacers, and adjust if necessary. Then place the last two washers over the rods, and tighten the nuts to lock the assembly together.

17. Cover the tension rods by using finishing screws to attach the last two seat slats to the outer spacers on each side of the bench.

18. Turn the bench upside-down, and center a pair of lower supports across the width of the bench at each end. The supports should be spaced 1-1/2" apart and 3-1/2" in from each end (directly over the spacers).

19. Complete the bench by fastening the supports in place with No. 10 x 2-1/2" deck screws inserted through the pre-drilled holes.

20. Place the bench over two Cube Planters, hooking the lower supports over the planters' edges.

MODULAR PLANTER
AND BENCH ENSEMBLE

SUGGESTED TOOLS

Circular saw
Hammer
Chisel
3/8" electric drill
Screwdriver
Table saw with dado blade
Router (optional)

MATERIALS LIST

(1) 1 x 12 x 8' Raised panels
(1) 2 x 4 x 8' Upper and lower rails
(1) 2 x 4 x 6' Corner posts and stiles

HARDWARE & SUPPLIES

Sandpaper
Quick-drying epoxy resin
(24) 1" finishing screws

Recommended Material and Finish:
redwood and water sealer

CUBE PLANTER

RAISED PANELS
(see Cutting Sequence)

1. Rip the 8' 1 x 12 to a width of 10-3/8", and then cut it into eight 11-7/8" panel blanks.

2. Set the trim blade on the table saw at an angle of 8° off vertical and to a depth of 2-1/4". Adjust the fence so that it is 1/4" from the blade at the table surface.

3. Examine the panel blanks, and mark their best (face) sides.

4. Pass each panel through the table saw with its back side running along the fence. Thirty-two cuts will be required for the eight blanks.

5. Readjust the saw to a vertical position, with the blade riding 1/4" from the fence, at a depth of 1/2".

6. Pass all four edges of each panel through the blade at this new setting.

7. Sand the panels, and set them aside for future use.

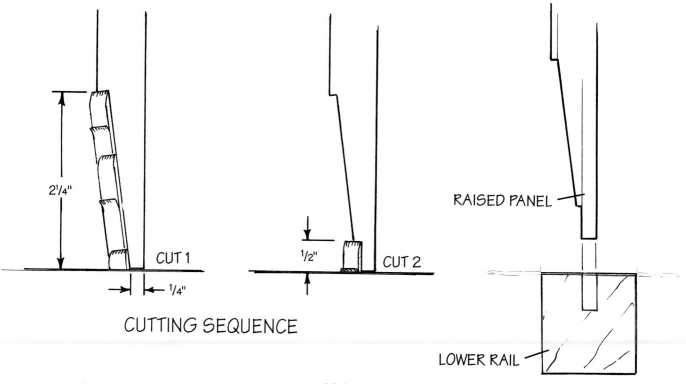

2¹/4"

1/4"

CUT 1

1/2"

CUT 2

RAISED PANEL

LOWER RAIL

CUTTING SEQUENCE

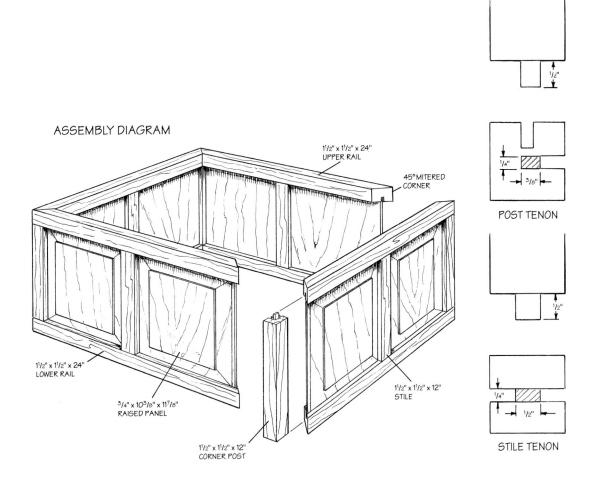

ASSEMBLY DIAGRAM

1½" x 1½" x 24"
UPPER RAIL

45°MITERED
CORNER

1½" x 1½" x 24"
LOWER RAIL

¾" x 10⅜" x 11⅞"
RAISED PANEL

1½" x 1½" x 12"
CORNER POST

1½" x 1½" x 12"
STILE

POST TENON

STILE TENON

PLANTER CONSTRUCTION

(see Assembly Diagram, Post Tenon, and Stile Tenon)

8. Set the table saw to rip at 1-1/2". Rip both 2 x 4s to yield a total of four 1-1/2" x 1-1/2" pieces of stock. Two passes through the saw will be required for each 2 x 4.

9. To make the eight upper and lower rails, cut two 24" lengths from each of the four pieces.

10. Cut 45° miters on both ends of every rail.

11. Cut four 1-1/2" x 1-1/2" x 12" corner posts and four stiles of the same dimensions from the remaining material.

12. Set the dado blade (or router bit) to cut a 1/4"-wide x 1/2"-deep groove.

13. Cut a groove down the center of two opposing faces of each of the four stiles.

14. On each of the four posts, make a similar cut down the center of two adjoining faces.

15. Make another similar cut on one face of each

upper and lower rail. Make sure this groove is on one of the two faces that is intersected by the 45° end miters.

16. On the end of each post, cut a 1/4" x 3/8" x 1/2"-long tenon, oriented in the same plane as the groove.

17. On the ends of each stile, cut a tenon 1/4" x 1/2" x 1/2".

18. Join each of the four panels with a center stile.

19. Place a mitered rail on the top and bottom edge of each raised-panel assembly so that the panels are centered.

20. Dry fit the entire assembly, making any necessary adjustments.

21. When the fit is satisfactory, fasten all joints and tenons with epoxy resin and 1" finishing screws inserted from the exterior faces, squaring the planter as you work. (Allow the panels to float within the frames.)

22. After the glue dries, sand all exposed surfaces.

23. Finish the planter with a colorless sealer.

105

BOOT BENCH

SUGGESTED TOOLS

Circular saw
Hand saw
Hammer
Mallet
Chisel
3/8" electric drill
Screwdriver
Table saw with dado blade
Router (optional)

MATERIALS LIST

(1) 1 x 12 x 6' Raised panels
(1) 2 x 8 x 6' Seat back sides
(1) 2 x 4 x 10' Rails, posts, stile, and cleats
(1) 1 x 6 x 10' Seat boards
(1) 1 x 6 x 6' Bench back and top slat
(1) 1/2" x 4' x 4' ext. plywood Bench bottom, back, and support strips

HARDWARE & SUPPLIES

Sandpaper
Quick-drying epoxy resin
No. 6 x 1-1/4" deck screws
6d finishing nails
(2) 3/4" x 3" hinges

Recommended Material and Finish:
redwood and water sealer

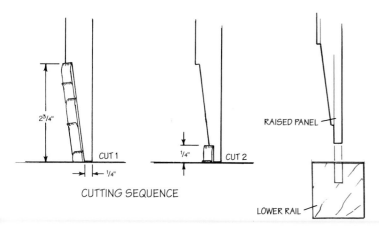

CUTTING SEQUENCE

RAISED PANELS

(see Assembly Diagram and Cutting Sequence)

1. Rip the 6' 1 x 12 to a width of 11-1/8".

2. From the ripped stock, cut two 16-1/4" and two 9-1/2" panel blanks.

3. Set the trim blade on the table saw at an angle of 8° off vertical and to a depth of 2-3/4". Adjust the fence so that it is 1/4" from the blade at the table surface.

4. Choose and mark the best (face) side of each panel blank.

5. Pass each blank through the table saw, with its back side riding along the fence. Sixteen cuts will be required for the four blanks.

6. Readjust the saw blade to a vertical position, with the blade riding 1/4" from the fence, at a depth of 1/4".

7. Pass all four edges of each blank through the blade at this new setting.

8. Sand the panels, and set them aside.

LEGS

(see Leg Pattern)

9. Cut two 3' leg blanks from the 6' 2 x 8.

10. Using the Leg Pattern illustration, lay out and cut two legs from the blanks. Note that each leg's full width is 7-1/4".

11. On the inside face of each leg, cut two full-width, 3/4"-deep x 1-1/2"-wide half-lap joints. The bottom of one joint should lie 3" from the bottom end of the leg; the top of the other should lie flush with the seat indentation.

12. Along the inside back face of each leg—from the base to the top of the upper half-lap joint—cut a 1/2"-wide and 3/4"-deep rabbet to accommodate the 1/2" plywood back.

13. Along the center of the front edges, cut or route a 1/4" x 1/4" groove from one half-lap joint to the other.

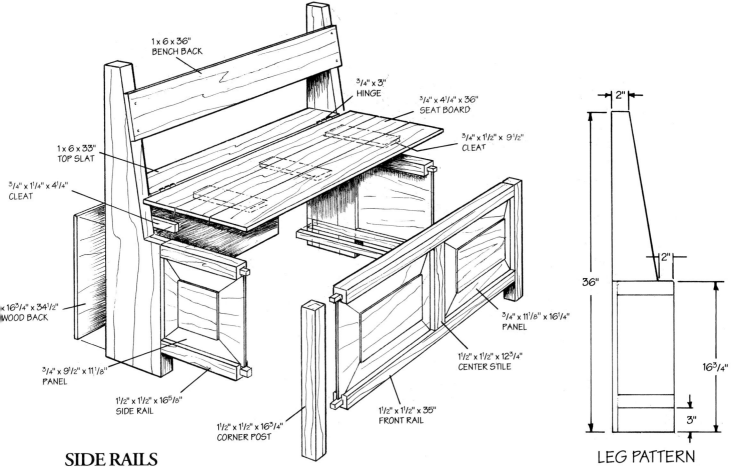

1 x 6 x 36"
BENCH BACK

³/₄" x 3"
HINGE

³/₄" x 4¹/₄" x 36"
SEAT BOARD

1 x 6 x 33"
TOP SLAT

³/₄" x 1¹/₂" x 9¹/₂"
CLEAT

³/₄" x 1¹/₄" x 4¹/₄"
CLEAT

x 16³/₄" x 34¹/₂"
WOOD BACK

³/₄" x 11¹/₈" x 16¹/₄"
PANEL

³/₄" x 9¹/₂" x 11¹/₈"
PANEL

1¹/₂" x 1¹/₂" x 12³/₄"
CENTER STILE

1¹/₂" x 1¹/₂" x 16⁵/₈"
SIDE RAIL

1¹/₂" x 1¹/₂" x 16³/₄"
CORNER POST

1¹/₂" x 1¹/₂" x 35"
FRONT RAIL

2"

2"

36"

16³/₄"

3"

LEG PATTERN

SIDE RAILS
(see Assembly Diagram)

14. Rip the 10' 2 x 4 into two 1-1/2" x 1-1/2"-wide blanks.

15. From each of the ripped pieces, cut two 16-5/8" side rails.

16. Down the center of one face of each rail, cut a 1/4" x 1/4" groove.

17. On one end of each rail, cut a 1/2" x 1/2" x 1"-long tenon.

18. On each rail's opposite end, cut a 1-1/2" x 6-1/2" half-lap joint. Be sure to orient these half-laps so that they are on opposing faces of the two pairs of rails.

CORNER POSTS AND SIDE ASSEMBLY
(see Assembly Diagram)

19. From the ripped stock, also cut two 16-3/4" corner posts.

20. On two adjoining faces of each post, cut a total of four 1/2" x 1/2" x 1" mortises to accommodate the rail tenons. Locate one set of mortises 3-1/2" up from the bottom, and position the other set 1/2" down from the top.

21. On the same adjoining faces of both corner posts, cut or route a 1/4" x 1/4" groove between the mortises.

FRONT RAILS AND CENTER STILE
(see Assembly Diagram)

22. From the remaining ripped stock, cut two 35" front rails.

23. At both ends of each rail, cut a 1/2" x 1/2" x 1" tenon.

24. Cut a 1/4" x 1/4" centered groove along one complete face of each front rail.

25. In the center of these grooves, cut a 1/2" x 1/2" x 1"-long mortise to accommodate the tenon on the center stile.

26. From the remaining ripped stock, cut one 12-3/4" center stile.

27. Cut a 1/4" x 1/4" groove down two of the stile's opposing faces.

28. Then cut a 1/2" x 1/2" x 1" tenon on each of the stile's ends.

107

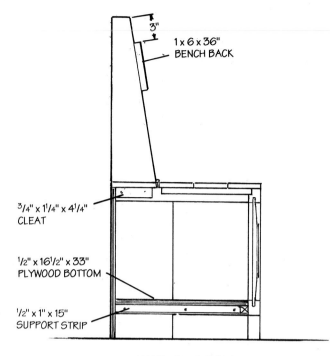

3"

1 x 6 x 36"
BENCH BACK

³/4" x 1¹/4" x 4¹/4"
CLEAT

¹/2" x 16¹/2" x 33"
PLYWOOD BOTTOM

¹/2" x 1" x 15"
SUPPORT STRIP

END SECTION

29. Check the fit of all mortises and tenons. You will need to bevel the ends of the rail tenons in order to keep them from hitting each other inside their mortises.

30. When the fit is satisfactory, glue the two side assemblies with epoxy resin, and set them aside to dry.

31. Next, glue and clamp the front rails and center stile to the side assemblies, placing the front panels within their frames.

SEAT BOARDS AND CLEATS
(see Assembly Diagram and End Section)

32. While the bench is drying, rip the 10' 1 x 6 to a width of 4-1/4".

33. Cut three 36" seat boards from the 4-1/4" piece.

34. From the scrap material, rip and cut three 3/4" x 1-1/2" x 9-1/2" cleats.

35. Turn the seat boards upside-down on a flat work surface, and lay them out into a 12-3/4" x 36" bench seat.

36. Rest the cleats on the seat boards (see Assembly Diagram for correct placement), and attach them with 1-1/4" deck screws.

37. From scrap material, cut two more cleats, 3/4" x 1-1/4" x 4-1/4" long.

38. With deck screws, attach these two cleats to the inside faces of the legs, flush with the upper edges of the half-lap joints.

BENCH BACK AND TOP SLAT
(see Assembly Diagram)

39. From the 6' 1 x 6, cut one 36" bench back and one 33" top slat.

40. Attach the top slat between and flush with the back edges of the legs by nailing it to the 4-1/4" cleats.

41. Nail the 36" bench back to the angled portion of the legs, about 3" down from the top.

SUPPORT STRIPS, BENCH BOTTOM, AND PLYWOOD BACK
(see Assembly Diagram and End Section)

42. Position the seat assembly on top of the bench, and attach it to the top slat with two 3/4" x 3" hinges.

43. Cut one 1" x 33" and two 1" x 15" support strips from the 1/2" plywood.

44. Turn the bench over, and screw these support strips along the inner front and both sides, flush with the bottom of the lower rails.

45. From the 1/2" plywood, cut a 16-1/2" x 33" bench bottom.

46. Attach the bench bottom to the support strips with deck screws.

47. From the remaining plywood, cut a 16-3/4" x 34-1/2" back.

48. Fasten the back by placing it into the legs' rabbets and attaching it with deck screws.

49. Sand the bench, and finish it by applying two or three coats of water sealer.

BOOT BENCH

———————

Gratifying mornings in the garden shouldn't be followed by tedious afternoons of cleaning indoors, but they will be if you leave a trail of muddy footprints and earth-encrusted tools each time you track through the house. A strategically placed Boot Bench—right by the back door—is guaranteed to maximize your outdoor leisure and minimize your indoor chores. Sit in comfort while you change your shoes, and then toss them into the bench's compartment before they have a chance to sully that spotless kitchen floor. Stash your tools too; you'll know right where they are when you need them next.

SUGGESTED TOOLS

Circular saw
Hammer
Chisel
Screwdriver
Table saw with dado blade
Router (optional)

MATERIALS LIST

(2) 4 x 4 x 8' Front and back posts
(1) 2 x 8 x 6' Top shelf
(2) 2 x 4 x 8' Front and back rails
(4) 1 x 4 x 8' (Alternative front and
       back rail construction.
       See step 10a.)
(1) 2 x 4 x 12' Side rails and stabilizers
(1) 3/4" x 4'x 4' ext. plywood
       Work surface and lower shelf

HARDWARE & SUPPLIES

No. 6 x 1 1/4" deck screws
Quick-drying epoxy resin
Sandpaper
(60) (4" x 4" tiles with mastic
       and grout for optional surface.
       See steps 10b and 22a.)

Recommended Material and Finish:
pressure-treated spruce, pine, or
fir with exterior primer and paint

POSTS AND TOP SHELF
(see Assembly Diagram and Alternative Post Detail)

1. Make the two front posts by cutting a 36" section from each of the two 8' 4 x 4s. The remaining 5' sections will serve as the back posts.

2. Cut a 60" section from the 2 x 8 to form the top shelf.

3. With a circular saw, bevel the top of each 5' back post by making four 45° cuts, 1" from the top of the post. For another decorative design possibility, refer to the illustration.

4. On one face of each front and each back post, make two 3/4"-deep x 3-1/2"-wide notches. The first notch should be placed 4" from the bottom of each post. (Measure notch heights from bottom of post to bottom of notch.) The second should be 32-1/2" from the bottom of each post. To make a notch with a circular saw, first set the blade to the desired depth. Then make the two outermost cuts. Follow these with several passes, 3/8" to 1/2" apart. Clean the remaining material from the notch with a chisel.

5. On the same face of the two 5' back posts only, make an additional notch 1-3/4" deep x 1-1/2" wide and 47-1/4" from the bottom of the post.

6. The fourth and final notch on all posts will be 1-1/2" deep x 3-1/2" wide, and 18-1/4" from the bottom of the post, adjacent to the previously notched sides. Before making these final cuts, study the Assembly Diagram for correct placement on each post.

RAILS AND STABILIZERS
(see Assembly Diagram and Tile Work Surface)

7. Cut two 45" front rails and two 45" back rails from the two 8' 2 x 4s.

8. From the 12' 2 x 4, cut the four 21-1/4" side rails and the two 27" stabilizers.

9. Cut a 3/4" x 3/4" rabbet along one edge of each of the four front and back rails and along one edge of two side rails. This is best done with a table saw and dado blade or with a router. If you are using a hard or dense wood, you may need to make two or three passes with

ASSEMBLY DIAGRAM

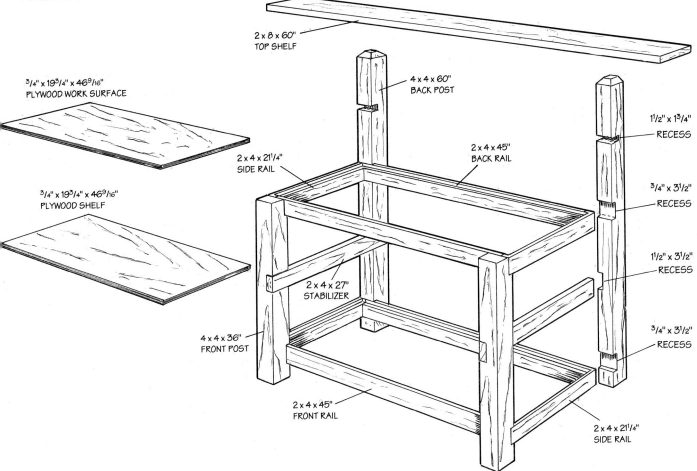

2 x 8 x 60"
TOP SHELF

3/4" x 19³/4" x 46⁹/16"
PLYWOOD WORK SURFACE

3/4" x 19³/4" x 46⁹/16"
PLYWOOD SHELF

4 x 4 x 60"
BACK POST

2 x 4 x 45"
BACK RAIL

1¹/2" x 1³/4"
RECESS

3/4" x 3¹/2"
RECESS

1¹/2" x 3¹/2"
RECESS

3/4" x 3¹/2"
RECESS

2 x 4 x 21¹/4"
SIDE RAIL

2 x 4 x 27"
STABILIZER

4 x 4 x 36"
FRONT POST

2 x 4 x 45"
FRONT RAIL

2 x 4 x 21¹/4"
SIDE RAIL

ALTERNATE POST DETAIL

3/4"

5¹/4"

6"

7"

TILE WORK SURFACE

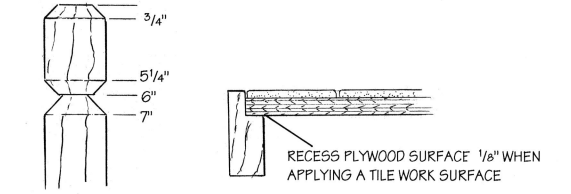

RECESS PLYWOOD SURFACE ¹/8" WHEN
APPLYING A TILE WORK SURFACE

POTTING BENCH

Potting plants is only messy or inconvenient when you don't have an organized area in which to work. If your plant containers are in the basement, your gardening tools in the garage, and your potting soil under the front steps, you'll find that this efficient and sturdy piece saves you a lot more time than it will take to build! Just fill its upper and lower shelves with everything you need, park it in a sheltered spot that's close to a water source, and say goodbye to those long afternoons of potting chaos.

the saw blade to remove the material.

10. Repeat this process with the other two side rails, but start and stop the cuts 3/4" from the rail ends. Clean up the rabbet ends with a chisel.

10a. If you only have access to a circular saw, you may wish to build most of your rails out of 1 x 4 stock. Rip inner pieces to a width of 2-3/4" prior to laminating them to outer pieces. When they're glued together, these will provide ready-made rabbets.

10b. If you want to tile the top of your potting bench, increase the rabbet depth on all top rails to 1-1/8". This cut will create a retaining lip around the work surface.

ASSEMBLY, WORK SURFACE, AND LOWER SHELF
(see Assembly Diagram)

11. Lay the two back posts down on the floor or on a low work surface. Make sure that the surface of each post that faces up has three notches and that the surfaces with single notches face each other.

12. Place the two 45" back rails into the two 3/4" x 3-1/2" notches in the back posts, with their rabbets facing up and in toward the center of what will be the completed bench. Position both rails so that they rest in the notches 1-1/2" in from the outer faces of each back post. (Use a scrap 2 x 4 as a spacer if necessary.)

13. Fasten the two rails in place with epoxy and 1-1/4" deck screws.

14. Slide the 2 x 8 top shelf into the upper notches of the back posts, center it, and fasten it with deck screws driven in at an angle from under the shelf.

15. Place the lower (fully rabbeted) rails in the lowest notches on the back posts, with their rabbets facing inside and up. Fasten these rails to the lower back rail with epoxy and deck screws.

16. Repeat this process with the upper (partly rabbeted) side rails.

17. Repeat steps 11, 12, and 13 with the two 36" front posts and front rails.

18. Tilt the front and back sections into upright positions. If necessary, use a 4" temporary block to hold the lower side rails horizontal.

19. Join the two sections at the notches, and fasten with epoxy and screws.

20. Slide the two side stabilizers into the 1-1/2" x 3-1/2" notches, and attach them with epoxy and screws.

21. Cut two panels measuring 46-9/16" x 19-3/4" from the 3/4" plywood to form the lower shelf and upper work surface.

22. Set both shelves into the rabbeted rail assemblies, and attach with epoxy and screws.

22a. If you plan to tile your work surface, first lay out the tile, and make any necessary cuts. Then spread a layer of mastic over the plywood, and position each tile. After the tiles have set (approximately 24 hours), the seams may be grouted.

23. If you'd like a slatted lower shelf instead of a solid one, use 1 x 4 slats (with 3/16" spaces between them) instead of plywood.

24. Sand the assembled bench.

25. Finish with exterior primer and two coats of exterior latex or enamel paint.

PAUSING IN THE PRESENT

In today's busy world, we move forward with tremendous speed and remarkable efficiency. So adept are we at racing through our daily schedules that where we started and where we're headed often become more important than where we are. If you find yourself marching through your yard (or life) from point A to point B without enjoying the space or time in between, now is the time—and your garden is the space—in which to pause in the present. Whether you've just rushed home from a busy day at the office or have finally finished planting the tomatoes, taking a break from goal-oriented activities will refresh your spirit and renew your soul. All you need is the outdoor furniture that will encourage you to relish a healing moment in the open air.

Every project in this section was designed to remind you to slow down, relax, and enjoy. From the Traditional Slab Bench to its magnificent English cousin, these bench and chair projects offer comfort, clean lines, and classic style. Pair either of the two, easily built coffee tables with any of the seats; you'll find that they come in handy. And then indulge in a well-deserved respite from everyday stress; sit down, breathe deeply, and savor the here-and-now.

TRADITIONAL SLAB BENCH

SUGGESTED TOOLS

Circular saw
Jigsaw
Hammer
Chisel
3/8" electric drill
Depth stop
Try square
Compass
Table saw with dado blade
   (optional)
Router (optional)

MATERIALS LIST

(1) 2 x 12 x 10' Seats, legs, and
   stretchers

HARDWARE & SUPPLIES

Sandpaper
Quick-drying epoxy resin

Recommended Material and Finish:
  pressure-treated spruce, pine, or fir with exterior
  primer and paint

CONSTRUCTION PROCEDURE
(see Assembly Diagram and Front View)

1. To form the legs, first cut two 19" lengths from the 10' 2 x 12.

2. With a compass, draw a 2-5/8" radius half-circle at the bottom center of each leg.

3. Cut the half-circles out with a jigsaw.

4. At the opposite end of each leg, use either a circular saw or a table saw with dado blade to cut a 1" x 1" x 10" tenon.

5. Form the seat by cutting a 44-1/4"-long section from the 2 x 12.

6. Rest the seat on your work surface so that the growth rings (visible in the end grain) cup up.

7. Using a square, lay out two 1" x 1" x 10" mortises, 8-1/2" in from each end of the seat, and centered between the seat's two long edges. The mortises should measure 26-1/4" from center to center.

8. Use either a router or a drill (with a 1" bit and depth stop) to remove most of the material from the mortise. Remove the remaining wood with a hammer and chisel. (For a clean cut, first score around the entire perimeter of the mortise with light blows to the chisel.)

FRONT VIEW

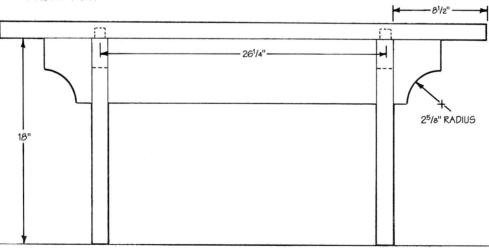

ASSEMBLY DIAGRAM

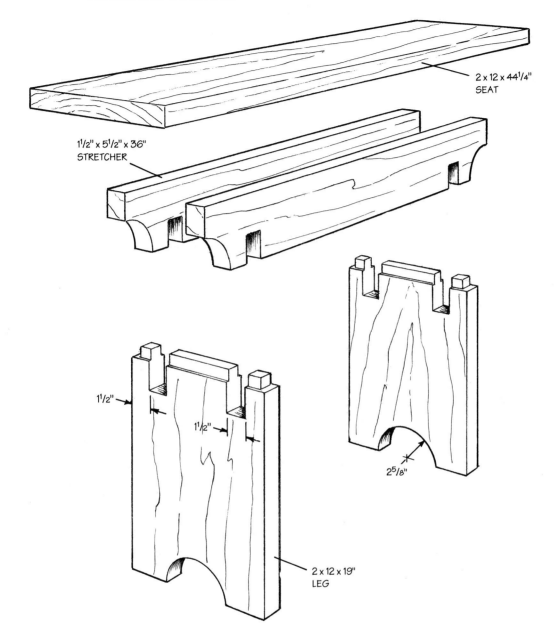

2 x 12 x 44 1/4"
SEAT

1 1/2" x 5 1/2" x 36"
STRETCHER

1 1/2"

1 1/2"

2 5/8"

2 x 12 x 19"
LEG

9. Dry fit the legs to the seat bottom, and make any necessary adjustments.

10. Remove the seat, and at the top of each leg, cut a pair of 1-1/2" x 1-1/2" x 3-1/2" notches located 1-1/2" in from each edge.

11. From the remaining 2 x 12 stock, rip two 1-1/2" x 5-1/2" boards.

12. From these two lengths, cut two 36"-long stretchers.

13. With a compass, draw a 2-5/8" radius quarter-circle at the bottom, outside corner of each stretcher.

14. Cut these quarter-circles out with a jigsaw.

15. Along the bottom edge of each stretcher, make two notches. Each notch should be 1-1/2" wide and 4-1/8" in from the end. Adjust the depth of the notch so that 2-1/2" of material is left after notching.

16. Sand all components.

17. Apply epoxy resin to all mortises, tenons, and to the top of both stretchers. Assemble and allow to dry.

18. After the epoxy has dried, seal the bench with exterior primer, and then apply two coats of exterior latex or enamel paint.

117

TRADITIONAL
SLAB BENCH

Many traditional furniture styles are characterized by simplicity of design, sturdiness, and ease of assembly. You'll find that this unassuming but attractive bench is no exception. Though it isn't flimsy, it is portable; when the sun's glare gets too bright in one place, just move your bench into the shade. During the coldest winter months, you might even want to touch up its paint and find your bench a vacation spot—indoors.

DUCKBOARD
BENCH

SUGGESTED TOOLS

Circular saw
Hack saw
3/8" electric drill
Screwdriver
Table saw with dado blade (optional)

MATERIALS LIST

(12) 1 x 4 x 6' Seat slats and spacers
(1) 4 x 4 x 6' Legs
(1) 3/8" x 36" All-thread tension rod
(1) 1 x 4 x 12' (Alternative leg construction. See step 5a.)
(2) 1 x 4 x 8's (Alternative leg construction. See step 5a.)

HARDWARE & SUPPLIES

(4) 3/8" nuts with washers
(8) 1" finishing screws
Sandpaper

Recommended Material and Finish:
redwood and water sealer

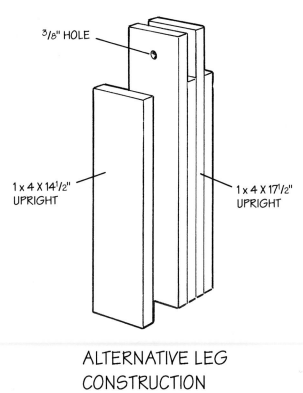

3/8" HOLE

1 x 4 X 14¹/₂"
UPRIGHT

1 x 4 X 17¹/₂"
UPRIGHT

ALTERNATIVE LEG CONSTRUCTION

SPACERS, LEGS, AND SLATS

(see Assembly Diagram, 4 x 4 Leg Detail, and Alternative Leg Construction)

1. Cut twelve 1 x 4 x 3-1/2" spacers from one of the 6' 1 x 4s.

2. From 1 x 4 scrap wood, cut a template 7" long, and drill a 3/8" pilot hole through it, centered 1-3/4" in from one end and 5-1/4" in from the other end.

3. Next, cut four 17-1/2" leg blanks from the 6' 4 x 4.

4. Make a center slot 3/4" wide x 3" deep across the top and center of each of the four legs.

5. Make another slot of equal depth 3/4" to each side of and parallel to the original cut. These cuts will extend past (and remove part of) two outer faces on each leg.

5a. An alternative leg construction is possible. Instead of slotting a 4 x 4, each leg can be built from 1 x 4s. To do this, cut eight 17-1/2" sections from a 1 x 4 x 12', and cut twelve 14-1/2" sections from two 1 x 4 x 8' boards. Then laminate these sections together to form four legs.

6. Using the template, drill a 3/8" hole, 1-3/4" up from the bottom of the slots through the center of the double tenon on each leg.

7. Use the same template to drill a countersink in the center of four of the spacer blocks; this should be large enough to accommodate a 3/8" nut and washer.

8. Next, check the length of the remaining eleven 6' 1 x 4s—the seat slats—and trim if necessary.

9. Using the template, drill a 3/8" hole at each end of nine of the eleven slats. Be sure that the pilot hole is centered 5-1/4" from the end of each slat.

10. Use the template again to drill 3/8" center holes in each of the twelve spacers.

11. Sand and seal all components, and then set them aside.

12. With a hacksaw, cut two 14-1/4" pieces from the tension rod. (You can save yourself some time by making both cuts through the tension rod's center section. Each of the two pieces you cut will have one end that

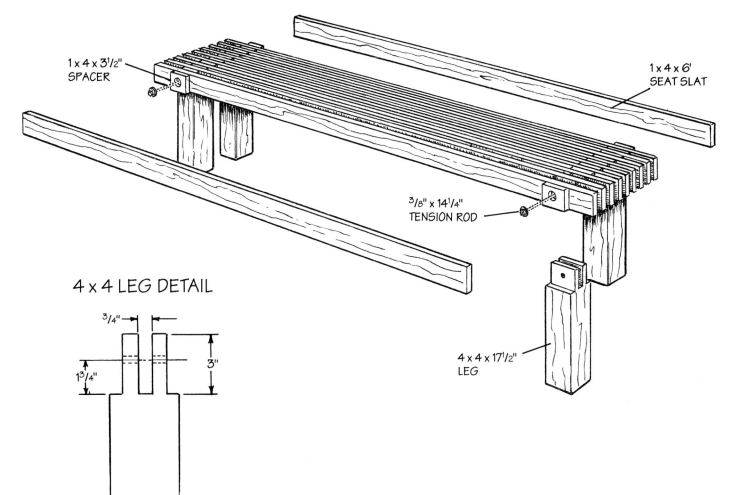

1 x 4 x 3½"
SPACER

1 x 4 x 6'
SEAT SLAT

³/₈" x 14¼"
TENSION ROD

4 x 4 x 17½"
LEG

4 x 4 LEG DETAIL

¾"

3"

1¾"

the hack saw hasn't touched—one end from which you won't have to file burrs!)

ASSEMBLY
(see Assembly Diagram)

13. Thread a nut onto (and flush with the cut end of) each rod.

14. Slide a washer over the opposite end of each rod, down to the nut.

15. Slide two of the four countersunk spacers onto the rods, with their countersinks facing the nuts and washers.

16. Place one bench slat on top of the spacers by sliding it over the rods.

17. You may need to enlist a helper for this step. Take one of the bench slats, and align the holes at each end with the holes in the double tenons of two legs.

18. Then slide this assembly over the tension rods.

19. Add another slat to the tension rods. Continue the alternating spacer-slat sequence until you've added four more slats. (You've now added a total of seven slats.)

20. Insert another leg-and-slat assembly.

21. Follow the assembly with a slat and then with the last, countersunk spacers, making sure that these are placed on the rods with their countersinks facing outward.

22. Check the alignment of all the spacers and legs, and adjust if necessary.

23. Place the last two washers over the rods, and tighten the last two nuts over them to lock the assembly together.

24. Cover the visible tension rod nuts with the remaining two seat slats. Position the ends of the slats, and then attach them with 1" finishing screws.

DUCKBOARD BENCH

This distinctive bench sheds water as efficiently as its feathered namesake; its vertically aligned seat slats won't retain potentially damaging moisture. The bench's design is elegant too. Internal parts—tension rods, nuts, and washers—are cleverly hidden by exterior slats to create a clean-lined style. If this look appeals to you, you'll also want to try the Modular Planter and Bench Ensemble; a nearly identical bench (one without legs) is modified to hook over the edges of two handsome planters.

CHIPPENDALE CHAIR

SUGGESTED TOOLS

Circular saw
Hammer
Mallet
Chisel
Level
3/8" electric drill
Jigsaw
Band saw (optional)
Table saw with dado blade (optional)

MATERIALS LIST

(1) 1/4" x 1' x 2' plywood Jig
(1) 3/4" x 1-1/4" x 9' Stiles and lattice slats
(1) 1/4" x 5-1/4" x 36" plywood Rear leg pattern
(1) 1-3/4" x 5-1/4" x 6' Rear legs
(2) 1-3/4" x 2-1/2" x 6' Front legs and rails
(1) 1-3/4" x 3-1/2" x 4' Arms
(1) 1-3/4" x 1-3/4" x 3' Stretchers
(1) 1" x 2-1/2" x 4' Upper and lower seat backs
(1) 1" x 2-1/2" x 10' Seat slats

HARDWARE & SUPPLIES

Quick-drying epoxy resin
6" of 1/4" dowel
(6) 1" finishing screws
Sandpaper

Recommended Material and Finish:
red oak and polyurethane

SEAT BACK
(see Panel Assembly)

1. From the piece of scrap 1/4" plywood, cut a jig measuring 18-1/2" wide x 12" tall.

2. Cut four 1-1/8" square plywood spacers from the remaining plywood.

3. Glue two spacers along each long edge of the jig, 1-1/4" in from the short ends.

4. From the 3/4" x 1-1/4" x 9' stock, cut two 13-1/2" stiles, squared at both ends.

5. From the remaining material, make the lattice slats by cutting (a) two 16-15/16" pieces, measured from the long point to the short point of parallel 45° cuts; (b) two 8-7/8" pieces, measured from the squared end to the long end of a 45° cut; (c) two 6" pieces, measured from the squared end to the long end of a 45° cut; (d) two 5" pieces, measured from the squared end to the long end of a 45° cut.

6. Starting with the two 16-15/16" center-support lattice slats (and using the Panel Assembly illustration as a placement guide), position the slats in the jig.

7. Cut half-lap joints at each intersection.

8. Dry fit all joints, and make adjustments as necessary.

PANEL ASSEMBLY

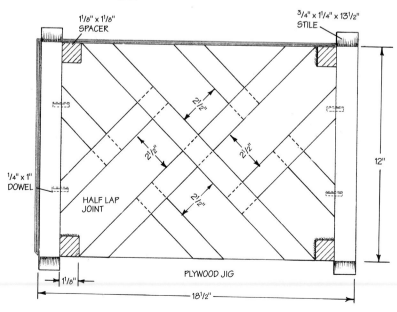

124

9. Glue all half-lap joints with epoxy resin, and allow to dry.

10. Next, cut a 1/4" x 3/4" x 1-1/8" tenon on both ends of each of the two 13-1/2" stiles.

11. Drill eight 1/4"-wide and 1/2"-deep holes (as shown in the Panel Assembly illustration), and fasten the stiles to the lattice with four 1" dowels, two in each stile. Set the panels aside.

REAR LEGS
(see Rear Leg Detail)

12. Next, you'll need to lay out the rear leg pattern on a piece of 1/4" x 5-1/4" x 36" plywood. Place the plywood in front of you, on a level surface, so that its long sides run up and down. Measure and draw a straight, vertical line, 17-1/2" long and 2-1/2" from the left side of the blank.

13. From the 17-1/2" point, angle the line back approximately 8°, and continue it until it intersects with the upper right-hand corner of the plywood blank.

14. Return to the point at which the line changed course (at 17-1/2"). From the edge of the plywood opposite to that point, draw a straight line parallel to the angled line and 2-1/2" away from it. Cut the leg pattern out.

15. Cut the 1-3/4" x 5-1/4" x 6' stock in half, and transfer the rear leg pattern to each half.

16. With a jigsaw, cut out the two rear leg blanks.

17. Lay out and cut the six mortises in each rear leg. Be sure to refer to the Rear Leg Detail and to the Assembly Diagram for correct mortise placement.

FRONT LEGS
(see Front Leg Detail and Assembly Diagram)

18. From each of the 1-3/4" x 2-1/2" x 6' pieces, cut a 25-1/2" front leg blank.

19. Lay out and cut the three mortises and one tenon on each leg. Refer to the illustrations for correct placement.

FRONT, BACK, AND SIDE RAILS
(see Assembly Diagram)

20. From each of the two remaining pieces of 1-3/4" x 2-1/2" stock, cut a 20-5/8" section to form the front and back rails, and a 17" section to form the side rails.

21. Cut a 1/2" x 1" x 2" tenon on the end of each of the four rails.

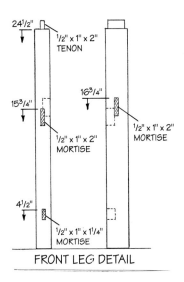

FRONT LEG DETAIL

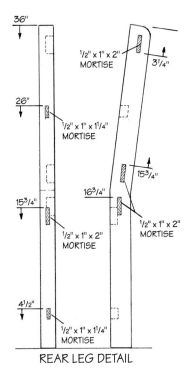

REAR LEG DETAIL

125

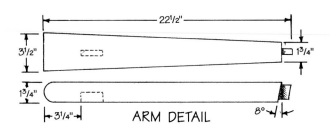

ARM DETAIL

22½"

3½"

1¾"

1¾"

3¼"

8°

ARMS

(see Arm Detail)

22. Cut two 22-1/2" arm blanks from the 4' section of 1-3/4" x 3-1/2" stock.

23. With a jigsaw, taper both edges of each arm from the full 3-1/2" width to 1-3/4".

24. Round the wide end of the arm by cutting a 1-3/4" radius half-circle, or choose one of the arm treatments shown with the Chippendale Bench.

25. Finish each arm by cutting a 1/2" x 1" x 1-1/4" tenon on the narrow end and a 1/2" x 1" x 2" mortise, 3-1/4" back from the front edge. Note that the narrow end of the arm is tapered at an 8° angle from the tenon.

STRETCHERS AND SEAT BACKS

(see Assembly Diagram)

26. From the 1-3/4" x 1-3/4" x 3' stock, cut two 17" stretchers.

27. At both ends of each stretcher, cut a vertical 1/2" x 1" x 1-1/4" tenon.

28. From the 1" x 2-1/2" x 4' piece of stock, cut two 20-5/8" seat backs (upper and lower).

29. Cut 1/2" x 1" x 2" tenons on both ends of each seat back.

30. Place the two seat backs on a work surface so that they are parallel and separated by a distance of 12".

31. Center the lattice panel between the seat backs.

32. Mark the location of the four stile tenons, and cut corresponding mortises in the backs.

33. Dry fit the panel and backs, make any necessary adjustments, and then glue the assembly together with epoxy resin.

34. Fasten the lattice work to the upper and lower seat backs with finishing screws.

SEAT

(see Assembly Diagram)

35. Cut the 1" x 2-1/2" x 10' piece of stock into five 22-1/4" seat slats.

36. Sand all components.

37. Dry fit the entire seat, making adjustments as necessary.

38. Assemble the seat (minus seat slats) with quick-drying epoxy resin, and allow to dry.

39. When the resin has cured, space the slats equally across the side rails, and epoxy them in place.

40. Complete the seat by applying two coats of polyurethane.

ASSEMBLY DIAGRAM

1" x 2½" x 20⅝"
UPPER SEAT BACK

12" x 18½"
LATTICE PANEL

1¾" x 3½" x 22½"
ARM

1" x 2½" x 22¼"
SEAT SLAT

1¾" x 2½" x 20⅝"
FRONT RAIL

1¾" x 2½" x 17"
SIDE RAIL

1¾" x 2½" x 25½"
FRONT LEG

1¾" x 5¼" x 36"
REAR LEG

1¾" x 1¾" x 17"
STRETCHER

126

CHIPPENDALE CHAIR

The Chippendale pattern on this chair's back looks deceptively complex, but trust us. We've done the math for you. All you have to do is cut the lattice strips to size, pop them in a jig, and presto! You'll have panels that will fit not only your chair but the Chippendale Bench too. The lattice design is also similar in style to the one on the Chippendale-Panel Planter; a grouping of all three projects will add a special touch to any garden location.

CHIPPENDALE
BENCH

SUGGESTED TOOLS

Circular saw
Chisel
Level
3/8" electric drill
Jigsaw
Band saw (optional)
Table saw with dado blade (optional)

MATERIALS LIST

(1) 1/4" x 2 x 2' plywood Jig
(3) 3/4" x 1-1/4" x 9' Panel stiles and
     lattice slats
(1) 1/4" x 5-1/4" x 36" plywood Rear
     leg pattern
(1) 1-3/4" x 5-1/4" x 6' Rear legs
(2) 1-3/4" x 2-1/2" x 9' Front legs and
     rails
(1) 1-3/4" x 3-1/2" x 4' Arms
(1) 1-3/4" x 1-3/4" x 6' Stretchers
(7) 1" x 2-1/2" x 6' Seat backs and slats

HARDWARE & SUPPLIES

Quick-drying epoxy resin
2' of 1/4" dowel
(18) 1" finishing screws
Sandpaper

Recommended Material and Finish:
   red oak and polyurethane

LATTICE PANELS
(see Panel Assembly)

1. From the piece of scrap 1/4" plywood, cut a jig measuring 18-1/2" wide x 12" tall.

2. Cut four 1-1/8"-square plywood spacers from the remaining plywood.

3. Glue two spacers along each long edge of the jig, 1-1/4" in from the short ends.

4. From each of the three pieces of 3/4" x 1-1/4" x 9' stock, cut two 13-1/2" stiles.

5. From the remaining 3/4" x 1-1/4" material, make the lattice slats by cutting (a) two 16-15/16" pieces, measured from the long point to the short point on parallel 45° cuts; (b) two 8-7/8" pieces, measured from the squared end to the long end of a 45° cut; (c) two 6" pieces, measured from the squared end to the long end of a 45° cut; (d) two 5" pieces, measured from the squared end to the long end of a 45° cut.

6. Starting with two 16-15/16" center-support lattice slats (and using the Panel Assembly illustration as a placement guide), position the lattice pairs in the jig.

7. Cut half-lap joints at each intersection.

PANEL ASSEMBLY

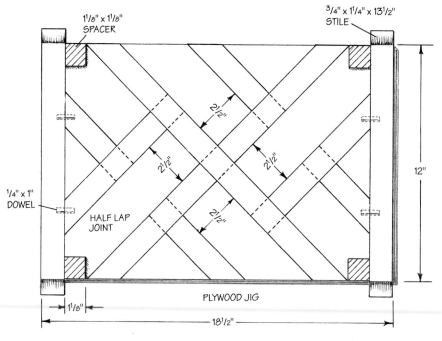

128

8. Dry fit all joints, and make adjustments as necessary.

9. Glue all half-lap joints with epoxy resin.

10. When the glued lattice work has dried, repeat this process to assemble two more sets of lattice work.

11. Next, cut a 1/4" x 3/4" x 1-1/8" tenon on both ends of each of the six 13-1/2" stiles.

12. Fasten two stiles to each lattice panel by drilling eight 1/4"-wide and 1/2"-deep holes (as shown in the Panel Assembly illustration) and inserting four 1" dowels, two in each stile.

13. Set the panels aside for later use.

REAR LEGS
(see Rear Leg Detail)

14. Next, you'll need to lay out the rear-leg pattern on a piece of 1/4" plywood measuring 5-1/4" x 36". Place the plywood in front of you, on a level surface, so that its long sides run up and down. Measure and draw a straight, vertical line, 17-1/2" long and 2-1/2" from the left side of the blank.

15. From the 17-1/2" point, angle the line back approximately 8°, and continue it until it intersects with the upper right-hand corner of the plywood blank.

16. Return to the point at which the line changed course (at 17-1/2"). From the edge of the plywood opposite to that point, draw a straight line parallel to the angled line and 2-1/2" away from it. Cut the leg pattern out.

17. Cut the 1-3/4" x 5-1/4" x 6' stock in half, and transfer the rear leg pattern to each half.

18. With a jigsaw, cut out the two rear leg blanks.

19. Lay out and cut the six mortises in each rear leg. Be sure to refer to the Rear Leg Detail and to the Assembly Diagram for correct mortise placement. You may also want to round the upper, outside corner of each leg.

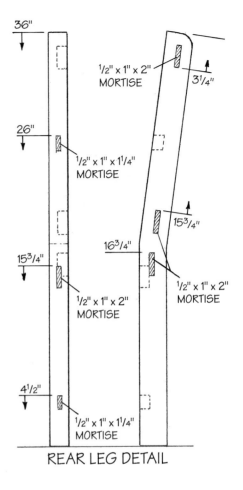

REAR LEG DETAIL

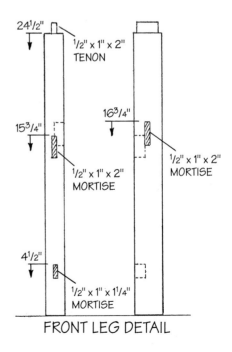

FRONT LEG DETAIL

CHIPPENDALE
BENCH

Though it makes a perfect complement to the Chippendale chair, this
handsome bench doesn't need help to
catch the eye. Its panels, constructed
with a homemade jig, aren't just
attractive; they're functional too—
tailored to keep your back cool on
those hot summer days when every
breeze feels like a gift from the heavens. And wherever you place this
bench, its natural color will blend
right in with the surroundings.

FRONT LEGS

(see Assembly Diagram and Front Leg Detail)

20. From each of the 1-3/4" x 2-1/2" x 9' pieces, cut a 25-1/2" front leg blank.

21. Lay out and cut the three mortises and one tenon on each leg. Refer to both the Front Leg Detail and to the Assembly Diagram for correct placement.

FRONT, SIDE, AND BACK RAILS

(see Assembly Diagram)

22. To form the front, back, and side rails, cut a 62" and a 17" section from each of the two remaining pieces of 1-3/4" x 2-1/2" stock.

23. Cut a 1/2" x 1" x 2" tenon on the end of each of the four rails.

24. Cut a 1/2" x 1 x 1-1/4" mortise in the center of each 62" rail.

ARMS

(see Arm Detail and Arm Variations)

25. Cut two 22-1/2" arm blanks from the 4' section of 1-3/4" x 3-1/2" stock.

26. With a jigsaw, taper both edges of each arm from the full 3-1/2" width to 1-3/4".

27. Round the wide end of the arm by cutting a 1-3/4" radius half-circle, or choose one of the other arm treatments.

28. Finish each arm by cutting a 1/2" x 1" x 1-1/4" tenon on the narrow end, and a 1/2" x 1" x 2" mortise, 3-1/4" back from the front edge. Note that in the Arm Detail, the narrow end of the arm is tapered at an 8° angle from the tenon to compensate for the slope of the rear leg.

STRETCHERS AND SEAT BACKS

(see Assembly Diagram)

29. From the 1-3/4" x 1-3/4" x 6' stock, cut two 17" stretchers and one 17-3/4" stretcher.

30. Cut a vertical 1/2" x 1" x 1-1/4" tenon on both ends of the two 17" stretchers and an offset, horizontal tenon of the same size on the ends of the 17-3/4" stretcher.

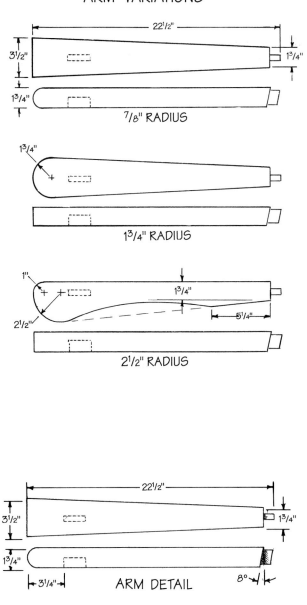

ARM VARIATIONS

7/8" RADIUS

1-3/4" RADIUS

2-1/2" RADIUS

ARM DETAIL

31. From the 1" x 2-1/2" stock, cut the two 62" seat backs (upper and lower).

32. Cut 1/2" x 1" x 2" tenons on the ends of each seat back.

131

33. Place the two backs on a work surface so that they are parallel and separated by a distance of 12".

34. Center the lattice panels between the seat backs so that equal distances separate them from each other and from the ends of the seat backs.

35. Mark the location of the twelve stile tenons, and cut corresponding mortises in the upper and lower seat backs.

36. Dry fit the panels and seat backs, make any necessary adjustments, and then glue the assembly together.

37. Fasten the lattice work to the upper and lower seat backs with finishing screws, using six screws per panel.

SEAT

(see Assembly Diagram)

38. Cut the remaining 6' 1" x 2-1/2" material into five 63-1/2" seat slats.

39. Sand all components.

40. Dry fit the entire bench, making adjustments as necessary.

41. Assemble the bench frame (minus seat slats) with quick-drying epoxy resin, and allow to dry.

42. When the resin has cured, space the slats at equal distances across the side rails, and epoxy them in place.

43. Complete the bench by applying two coats of polyurethane.

ASSEMBLY DIAGRAM

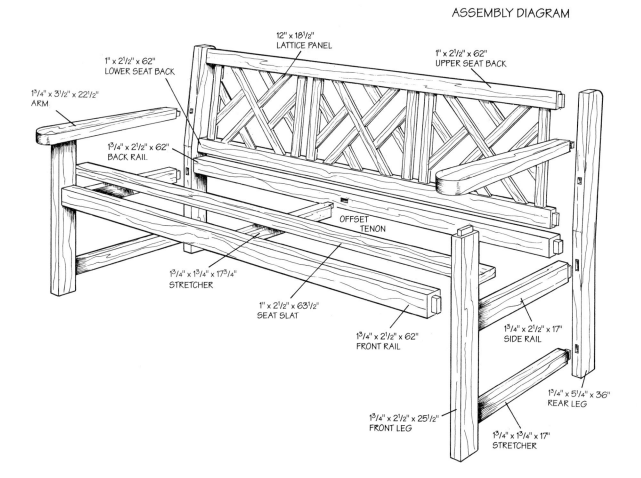

12" x 18¹⁄₂"
LATTICE PANEL

1" x 2¹⁄₂" x 62"
LOWER SEAT BACK

1" x 2¹⁄₂" x 62"
UPPER SEAT BACK

1³⁄₄" x 3¹⁄₂" x 22¹⁄₂"
ARM

1³⁄₄" x 2¹⁄₂" x 62"
BACK RAIL

OFFSET
TENON

1³⁄₄" x 1³⁄₄" x 17³⁄₄"
STRETCHER

1" x 2¹⁄₂" x 63¹⁄₂"
SEAT SLAT

1³⁄₄" x 2¹⁄₂" x 62"
FRONT RAIL

1³⁄₄" x 2¹⁄₂" x 17"
SIDE RAIL

1³⁄₄" x 2¹⁄₂" x 25¹⁄₂"
FRONT LEG

1³⁄₄" x 5¹⁄₄" x 36"
REAR LEG

1³⁄₄" x 1³⁄₄" x 17"
STRETCHER

COFFEE TABLE
(small)

SUGGESTED TOOLS

Circular saw
Hammer
Chisel
Screwdriver
3/8" electric drill
Try square
Router
Table saw with dado blade (optional)

MATERIALS LIST

(1) 4 x 4 x 6' Legs
(1) 1" x 3-1/2" x 8' Skirt boards and cleats
(2) 3/4" x 2" x 10' Top slats

HARDWARE & SUPPLIES

Quick-drying epoxy resin
No. 10 x 2-1/2" deck screws
No. 6 x 1-1/4" deck screws
Sandpaper

Recommended Material and Finish:
red oak and polyurethane

LEGS, SKIRT BOARDS, AND CLEATS

(see Assembly Diagram, Mortise and Tenon Detail, and Top View)

1. To form the legs, cut four 15-1/2" lengths, squared at both ends, from the 6' 4 x 4.

2. Cut four 15" skirt boards and two 17-1/2" cleats from the 8' section of 1" stock.

3. Lay out and cut a 1/2" x 1" x 2" offset tenon on each end of the four skirt boards.

4. On the upper edge of the face opposite the offset tenon, route a 1/8"-deep x 1/2"-wide rabbet along the full length of the skirt.

5. Examine the four legs, and determine which two faces will be exposed.

6. Along the top edge of these faces, route a 3/8"-deep x 1/2"-wide rabbet.

7. On each of the other faces, lay out a 1/2" x 1" x 2" mortise, 3/4" down from the top edge and 3/4" in from the exposed face. Remove the material with a drill and depth stop set at 1". Finish the joint with a hammer and chisel.

8. Dry fit the skirt boards and legs, and make any necessary adjustments. If cut correctly, the legs should have a 1/4" reveal, and the rabbets should form a continuous groove around the top perimeter of the table.

9. Apply epoxy resin to all the joints, and assemble the table frame and legs. For added holding power, 2-1/2" deck screws can be used to fasten each mortise and tenon joint from the concealed side of each post. Be sure to pre-drill the holes to prevent splitting.

10. Locate the cleats, and in one narrow edge of each, drill two holes, 3/8" wide, 1" deep, and 1-1/8" from each end.

11. Then, finish drilling through the boards with a 3/16" bit.

12. When the glued joints on the skirt and leg assembly have dried, insert 2-1/2" screws through the screw pockets to fasten the two cleats flush with the tops of the legs.

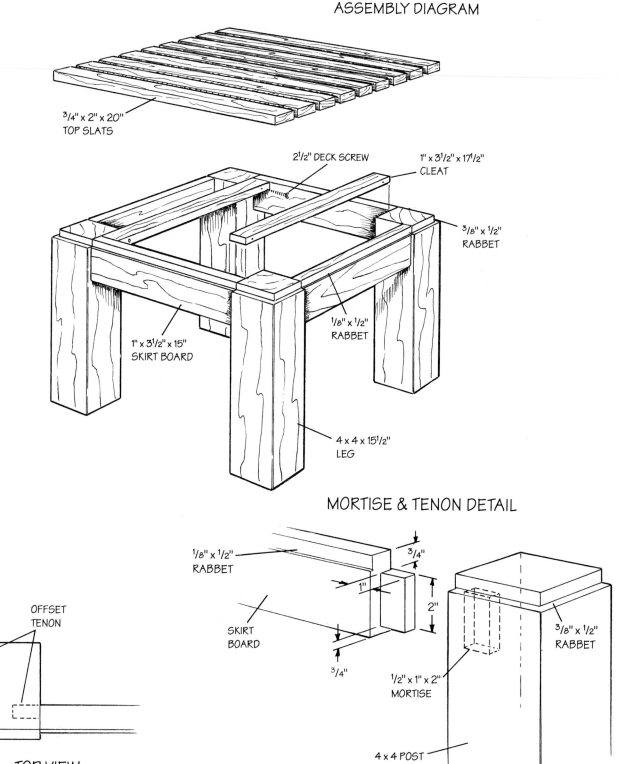

ASSEMBLY DIAGRAM

3/4" x 2" x 20"
TOP SLATS

2 1/2" DECK SCREW

1" x 3 1/2" x 17 1/2"
CLEAT

3/8" x 1/2"
RABBET

1/8" x 1/2"
RABBET

1" x 3 1/2" x 15"
SKIRT BOARD

4 x 4 x 15 1/2"
LEG

MORTISE & TENON DETAIL

1/8" x 1/2"
RABBET

3/4"

1"

2"

SKIRT
BOARD

3/4"

3/8" x 1/2"
RABBET

1/2" x 1" x 2"
MORTISE

4 x 4 POST

OFFSET
TENON

TOP VIEW

TOP SLATS AND ASSEMBLY
(see Assembly Diagram)

13. Cut nine 20" slats from the 3/4" x 2" x 10' boards.

14. Place the slats (with their best faces down) on a flat work surface, spacing them about 1/4" apart to form a 20" x 20" pattern.

15. Turn the leg assembly upside-down on top of the slats, making sure that the top is square and flush.

16. Drill pilot holes through the cleats into each slat.

17. Fasten the cleats to the slats with 1-1/4" screws.

18. Sand all surfaces and finish the assembled table with polyurethane.

134

COFFEE TABLE
(small)

No matter how stylish or comfortable your garden seating arrangements are, if you haven't included a table or two in the decor, you're likely to find that even a favorite bench or chair begins to lack appeal. Why? Because there's no place to put down that book you were reading, the refreshing drink in your hand, the sun bonnet, sandwich, or trowel. Thanks heavens for our favorite horizontal surface— the simple table-top! Just one garden table will bring you back to your bench or chair in no time at all, and two may bring a few guests as well. If you like this small project, try the medium-sized coffee table too; the two projects are designed to complement one another.

COFFEE TABLE
(medium)

SUGGESTED TOOLS

Circular saw
Hammer
Chisel
Screwdriver
3/8" electric drill
Try square
Router
Table saw with dado blade (optional)

MATERIALS LIST

(1) 4 x 4 x 6' Legs
(1) 1" x 3-1/2" x 14' Skirt boards and
   cleats
(3) 3/4" x 2" x 10' Top slats

HARDWARE & SUPPLIES

Quick-drying epoxy resin
No. 10 x 2-1/2" deck screws
No. 6 x 1-1/4" deck screws
Sandpaper

Recommended Material and Finish:
   red oak and polyurethane

LEGS, SKIRTS BOARDS, AND CLEATS
(see Assembly Diagram,
Mortise and Tenon Detail, and Top View)

1. To form the legs, cut four 15-1/2" lengths, squared at both ends, from the 6' 4 x 4.

2. From the 14' section of 1" stock, cut two 15" skirt boards, two 35" skirt boards, and three 17-1/2" cleats.

3. Lay out and cut a 1/2" x 1" x 2" offset tenon on each end of the four skirt boards.

4. On the upper edge of the face that is opposite to the offset tenon, route a 1/8"-deep x 1/2"-wide rabbet the full length of the skirt.

5. Examine the four leg blanks, and determine which two faces of each will be exposed.

6. Route a 3/8"-deep x 1/2"-wide rabbet along the top edges of these faces.

7. On each of the other two faces, lay out 1/2" x 1" x 2" mortise, 3/4" down from the top edge and 3/4" in from the exposed face. Remove the material with a drill and depth stop set at 1". Finish the joint with a hammer and chisel.

8. Dry fit the skirt boards and legs, and make any necessary adjustments. If cut correctly, the legs should have a 1/4" reveal, and the rabbets should form a continuous groove around the top perimeter of the table.

9. Apply epoxy resin to all joints, and assemble. For added holding power, 2-1/2" deck screws can be used to fasten each mortise and tenon joint from the concealed side of each post. Be sure to pre-drill holes for these screws, in order to prevent splitting.

10. Locate two of the cleats, and in one, long edge of each, drill two 3/8" holes, 1" deep, and 1-1/8" in from each end.

11. Then finish drilling through the boards with a 3/16" bit.

12. On the third cleat, drill two 1/8" toe-screw holes at each end.

13. When the joints on the skirt and leg assembly have dried, fasten the two outer cleats flush with the tops of the legs, using 2-1/2" screws inserted through the pre-drilled screw pockets.

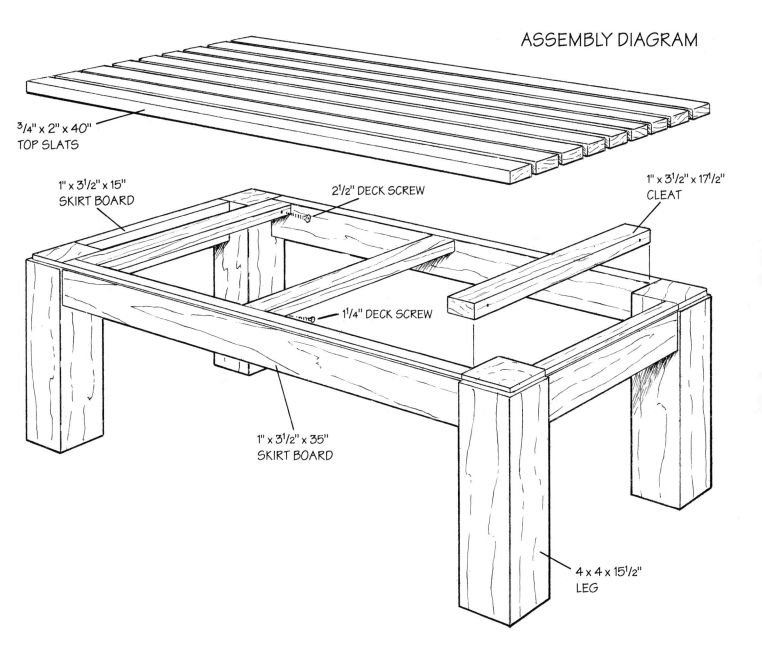

ASSEMBLY DIAGRAM

¾" x 2" x 40"
TOP SLATS

1" x 3¹/2" x 15"
SKIRT BOARD

2¹/2" DECK SCREW

1" x 3¹/2" x 17¹/2"
CLEAT

1¹/4" DECK SCREW

1" x 3¹/2" x 35"
SKIRT BOARD

4 x 4 x 15¹/2"
LEG

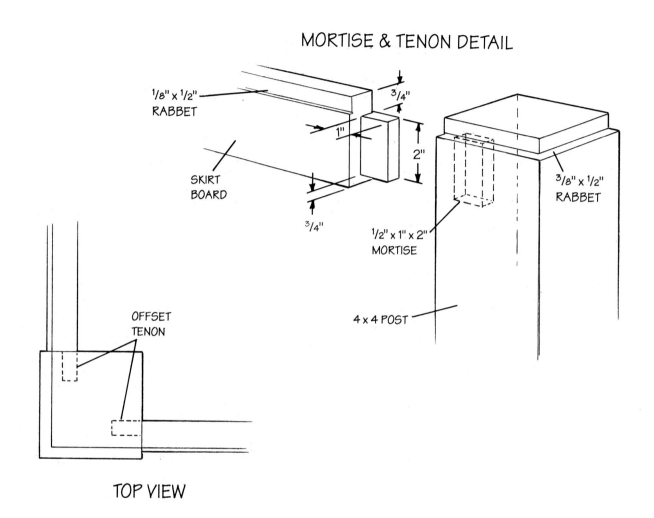

MORTISE & TENON DETAIL

1/8" x 1/2" RABBET

SKIRT BOARD

3/4"

1"

2"

3/4"

1/2" x 1" x 2" MORTISE

3/8" x 1/2" RABBET

4 x 4 POST

OFFSET TENON

TOP VIEW

14. Center the third cleat flush with the top of the two long skirt boards, and fasten it in place with two 1-1/4" deck screws, one in each end.

TOP SLATS AND ASSEMBLY
(see Assembly Diagram)

15. Lay out and cut the three 3/4" x 2" x 10' pieces into nine 40" top slats. (If your stock is exactly 10', allow for saw kerf loss; make the pieces equal in length and as long as possible.)

16. Place these tops slats—best face down—on a flat work surface, spacing them about 1/4" apart to form a 20" x 40" pattern.

17. Turn the leg assembly upside-down on top of the slats, making sure that the top is square and flush.

18. Drill a pilot hole through the cleats and into each slat.

19. Fasten the cleats to the slats with 1-1/4" screws.

20. Sand all surfaces, and finish the assembled table with polyurethane.

COFFEE TABLE
(medium)

Like the smaller coffee table, this project can be paired with any of the benches or chairs, but it's equally impressive when it stands alone. The simple but distinctive slatted top provides a functional surface for everything from gardening shears to a meal for two, and its sturdy legs will withstand years of use. Whether it finds its home on your patio, by your pool, or under the largest tree in your yard, this coffee table is likely to play a consistently pleasing role in your outdoor life.

ARCHED-BACK PAINTED CHAIR

SUGGESTED TOOLS

Circular saw
Hammer
Mallet
Chisel
Level
3/8" electric drill
Jigsaw
Band saw (optional)
Table saw with dado blade (optional)

MATERIALS LIST

(1) 2 x 8 x 6' Front and back legs
(1) 2 x 4 x 6' Side rails and stretchers
(1) 2 x 4 x 8' Front and back rails and arms
(1) 1 x 6 x 10' Back and seat slats

HARDWARE & SUPPLIES

Sandpaper
Quick-drying epoxy resin
(10) 1" finishing screws

Recommended Material and Finish:
pressure-treated spruce, pine, or fir with exterior primer and paint

FRONT AND BACK LEGS
(see Leg Detail and Mortise Guide)

1. Cut the 6' 2 x 8 in half.

2. Lay out a front and back leg on each half, using the Leg Detail as a guide, and then cut the legs out.

3. At the top of each front leg, notch out a 1/2" x 1"-long x 1-1/2" tenon.

4. Using the Mortise Guide, lay out and cut the required mortises—three in each front leg and eight in each back leg.

SEAT RAILS AND STRETCHERS
(see Assembly Diagram and Seat Rail Detail))

5. Form the contoured seat rails and the stretchers by cutting four 17-1/2" sections from the 6' 2 x 4.

6. Rip the two stretchers down to a width of 2-1/2".

7. Readjust the saw, and rip the seat rails to a width of 3-1/4".

8. On the end of each stretcher and rail, cut a 1"-long tenon, leaving a 1/2" shoulder at every side.

9. Lay out the curved pattern along the top edge of both seat rails.

10. Cut along the curve with either a band saw or a jigsaw.

FRONT AND BACK RAILS
(see Assembly Diagram)

11. From the 8' 2 x 4, cut a 21" front rail and a 21" back rail.

12. Cut a 1"-long tenon at the ends of each rail, leaving a 1/2" shoulder at each side.

ARMS
(see Assembly Diagram and Arm Layout)

13. On the remaining piece of 2 x 4, lay out two 22-1/2" arms, using the illustration as a guide. The narrow end's width will be 1-1/2" x 1-1/2" and the wide end will be 1-1/2" x 2-3/4".

14. Cut the arms out with a jigsaw.

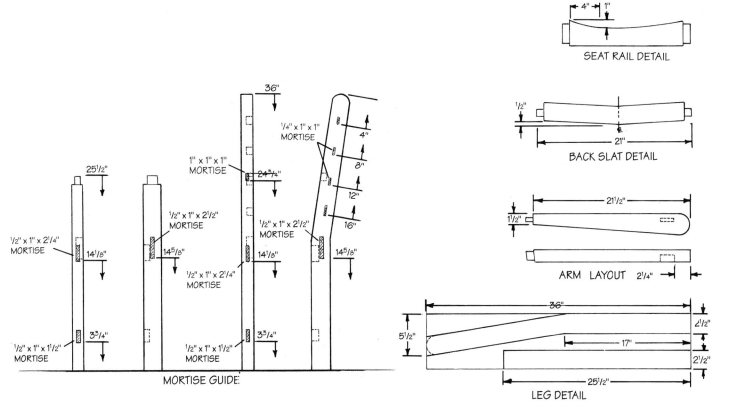

SEAT RAIL DETAIL

BACK SLAT DETAIL

ARM LAYOUT

LEG DETAIL

MORTISE GUIDE

15. At the tapered end of each arm, cut a 1"-long tenon, leaving a 1/4" shoulder at each side. Note that this end of the arm is angled slightly to compensate for the slanted back leg.

BACK SLATS AND SEAT SLATS
(see Assembly Diagram and Back Slat Detail)

16. First, rip a 3" strip off the 10' 1 x 6.

17. Cut four 21" back slats from that strip.

18. At each end of all slats, lay out and cut a 1/4" x 1" x 1" tenon, 1" from the lower edge.

19. After the tenons have been cut, lay out and cut the "V" pattern on each slat, using the Back Slat Detail as a guide.

20. Cut five 22" seat slats from the remaining 10' section.

ASSEMBLY
(see Assembly Diagram)

21. Dry fit all the components, and make any necessary alterations.

22. Mark the placement of the front leg tenon on the underside of each arm, and cut a corresponding mortise.

23. Sand all components.

24. Using epoxy resin, assemble the chair frame.

25. After the epoxy has dried, prime the frame and the seat slats with exterior primer.

26. When the primer has dried, use finishing screws to attach the equally-spaced seat slats along the curve of the side rails.

27. Finish the chair by applying two coats of exterior paint.

ASSEMBLY DIAGRAM

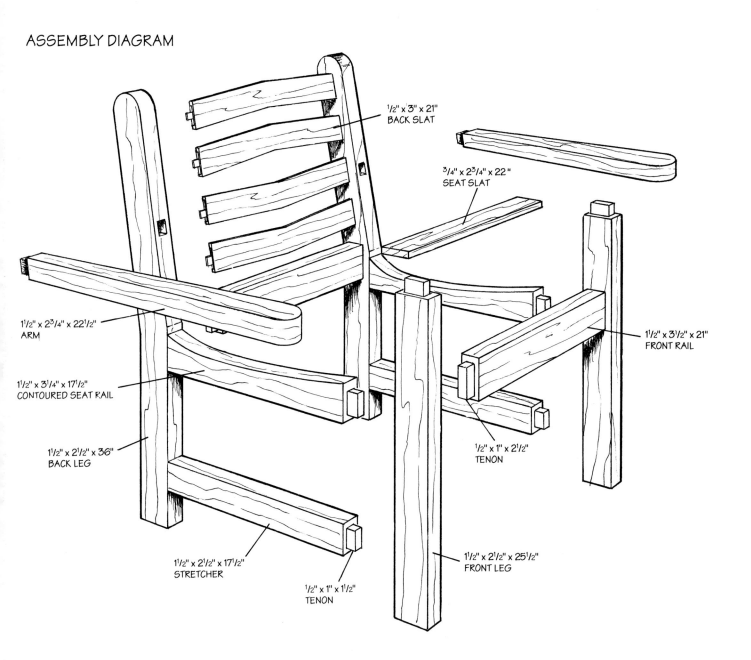

1/2" x 3" x 21"
BACK SLAT

3/4" x 2 3/4" x 22"
SEAT SLAT

1 1/2" x 2 3/4" x 22 1/2"
ARM

1 1/2" x 3 1/4" x 17 1/2"
CONTOURED SEAT RAIL

1 1/2" x 2 1/2" x 36"
BACK LEG

1 1/2" x 2 1/2" x 17 1/2"
STRETCHER

1/2" x 1" x 1 1/2"
TENON

1/2" x 1" x 2 1/2"
TENON

1 1/2" x 3 1/2" x 21"
FRONT RAIL

1 1/2" x 2 1/2" x 25 1/2"
FRONT LEG

ARCHED-BACK PAINTED CHAIR

The Arched-Back Painted Chair was designed to sit side-by-side with the Arched-Back Painted Bench—and to add a touch of garden color. But this distinctive chair will look equally impressive on its own or with a small table. And if you don't find painted surfaces appealing, just choose a wood that will accept a clear finish instead.

ARCHED-BACK PAINTED BENCH

SUGGESTED TOOLS

Circular saw
Hammer
Mallet
Chisel
Level
3/8" electric drill
Jigsaw
Band saw (optional)
Table saw with dado blade (optional)

MATERIALS LIST

(1) 2 x 8 x 6' Front and back legs
(1) 2 x 4 x 12' Seat rails, arms, and
    stretchers
(1) 2 x 4 x 10' Front and back rails
(2) 1 x 8 x 10' Back and seat slats
(1) 1 x 4 x 6' Seat slat

HARDWARE & SUPPLIES

Sandpaper
Quick-drying epoxy resin
(15) 1" finishing screws

Recommended Material and Finish:
  pressure-treated spruce, pine, or
  fir with exterior primer and paint

LEGS

(see Leg Detail, and Mortise Guide)

1. Cut the 6' 2 x 8 in half.

2. Using the Leg Detail as a guide, lay out a front and back leg on each half.

3. Cut out the four leg blanks.

4. Cut a 1"-long x 1/2" x 1-1/2" tenon at the top of each front leg.

5. Lay out and cut the required mortises—three in each front leg and eight in each back leg—using the Mortise Guide to determine correct placement.

SEAT AND CENTER RAILS, STRETCHERS, AND ARMS

(see Assembly Diagram, Seat Rail Detail, and Arm Layout)

6. To form two seat rails and two stretchers, first cut four 17-1/2" sections from the 12' 2 x 4.

7. Cut an additional 18-1/2" center seat rail from the same board.

8. Rip the two stretchers down to a width of 2-1/2".

9. Readjust the saw, and rip the rails to a width of 3-1/4".

10. Cut a 1"-long tenon at the end of each stretcher and rail, leaving a 1/2" shoulder at each side.

11. Lay out the curved pattern along the top edge of all three rails, and cut along the curves with either a jigsaw or a band saw. Note that because the center rail is 1" longer than the other two seat rails, there will be a 1/2" flat surface just in front of each tenon shoulder once the curved pattern has been transferred.

12. Using the Arm Layout as a guide, lay out two 22-1/2"-long arms on the remaining piece of the 12' 2 x 4.

13. Cut the arms out with a jigsaw. The narrow ends will be 1-1/2" and the wide ends will be 2-3/4".

14. At the narrow end of each arm, cut a 1"-long tenon, leaving a 1/4" shoulder on every side. Note that this end of the arm is angled slightly to compensate for the slanted back leg.

ARCHED-BACK PAINTED BENCH

Think of this impressive bench as an enlarged version of the Arched-Back Painted Chair because that's exactly what it is. Some of the component parts are longer of course, and you'll need to cut a few more mortises, but if you've successfully built the chair, you'll have no trouble constructing its handsome counterpart either.

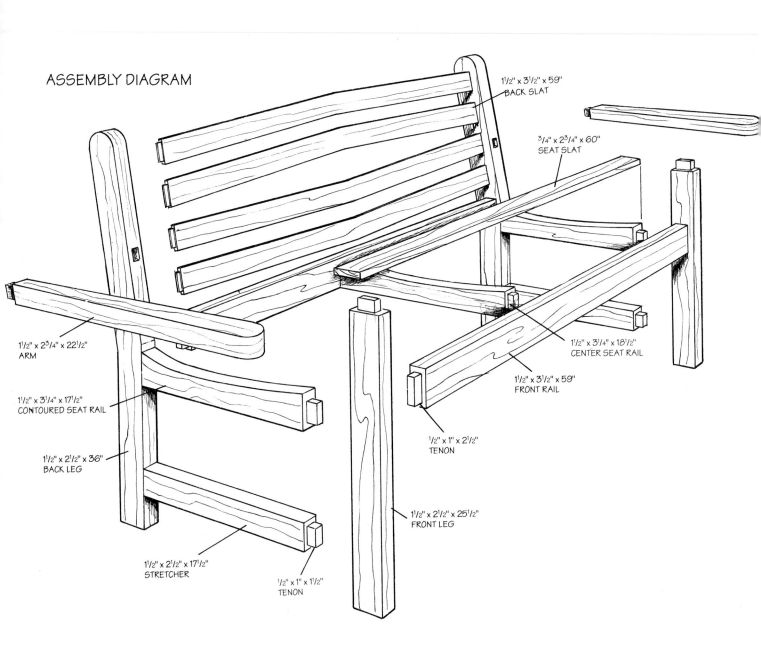

ASSEMBLY DIAGRAM

1½" x 3½" x 59"
BACK SLAT

¾" x 2¾" x 60"
SEAT SLAT

1½" x 2¾" x 22½"
ARM

1½" x 3¼" x 17½"
CONTOURED SEAT RAIL

1½" x 2½" x 36"
BACK LEG

1½" x 3¼" x 18½"
CENTER SEAT RAIL

1½" x 3½" x 59"
FRONT RAIL

½" x 1" x 2½"
TENON

1½" x 2½" x 25½"
FRONT LEG

1½" x 2½" x 17½"
STRETCHER

½" x 1" x 1½"
TENON

FRONT AND BACK RAILS

(see Assembly Diagram)

15. From the 10' 2 x 4, cut the two 59" front and back rails.

16. On the end of each rail, cut a 1"-long tenon, leaving a 1/2" shoulder on all four sides.

17. In the center of each 59" rail, 1/2" up from the lower edge, cut a 1/2" x 2-1/4" x 1"-deep mortise.

BACK SLATS

(see Assembly Diagram and Back Slat Detail)

18. Rip a 3-1/2" strip off each of the two 10' 1 x 8s.

19. Cut two 59" back slat blanks from each of the two strips.

20. At both ends of each blank, cut a 1/4" x 1" x 1" tenon, 1" from the lower edge.

21. Using the Back Slat Detail as a guide, lay out and cut the "V" pattern on each slat.

146

22. Rip the remaining 10' sections to a width of 2-3/4".

23. Then cut four of the five 60" seat slats from the ripped stock.

24. From the 6' 1 x 4, rip the last seat slat, cutting it to a length of 60".

25. Dry fit all the components, making adjustments as necessary.

26. Mark the placement of the front leg tenons on the undersides of the arms, and cut the corresponding mortises.

27. Sand all components.

28. Assemble the chair frame and back, using epoxy resin.

29. After the epoxy has dried, prime the frame and seat slats with exterior primer.

30. When the primer is dry, space the seat slats at an equal distance from one another across the curves of the seat rails, and use finishing screws to attach them to the seat rails.

31. Finish the bench by painting it with two coats of exterior grade paint.

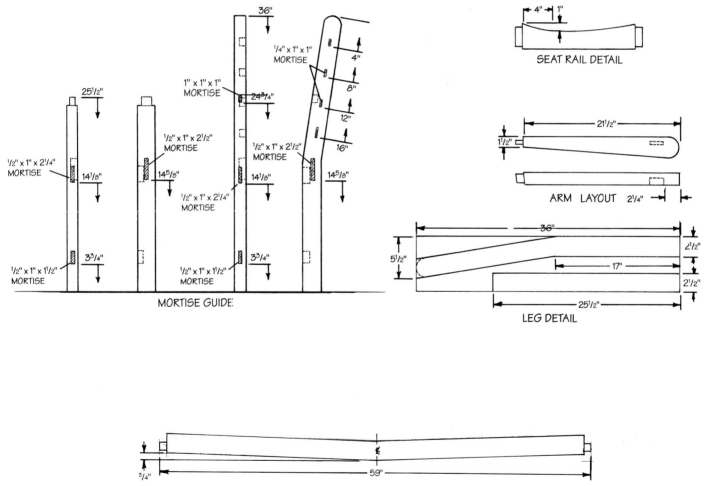

SEAT RAIL DETAIL

ARM LAYOUT

LEG DETAIL

MORTISE GUIDE

BACK SLAT DETAIL

BENCH BUILT
FOR TWO

You certainly don't have to be in love to own or enjoy this project, but if you can imagine yourself spooning with someone special, you might want to include a Bench Built for Two in the picture! Deceptively sedate and delightfully intimate, this two-seater is not especially difficult to construct and will reward you with years of use, whether you share it or enjoy it alone.

BENCH BUILT
FOR TWO

SUGGESTED TOOLS

Circular saw
Hammer
Chisel
3/8" electric drill
Jigsaw
Band saw (optional)
Table saw with dado blade (optional)

MATERIALS LIST

(1) 1-7/8" x 5-1/2" x 6' Rear uprights
(2) 1-7/8" x 5-1/2" x 6' Seat back rail,
    arms, front uprights, stretchers,
    and seat rails
(1) 1-7/8" x 3-1/4" x 4' Front rail
(3) 1" x 2-1/2" x 8' Seat slats
(1) 7/8" x 3" x 9' Back slats

HARDWARE & SUPPLIES

Quick-drying epoxy resin
2" brass panhead screws (10)
Sandpaper

Recommended Material and Finish:
  red oak and polyurethane

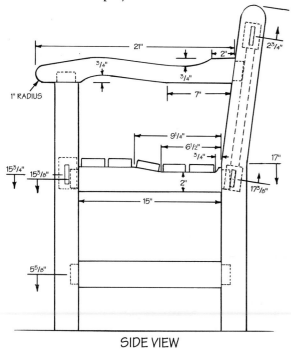

SIDE VIEW

CONSTRUCTION PROCEDURE
(see Assembly Diagram, Arm Detail, and Side View)

1. Before starting on the bench, transfer the arm pattern from the Arm Detail, and the seat rail and rear upright patterns from the Side View, to pieces of poster board or thin plywood. (The full length of the seat rail is 17"; the leg's height is 33", its width is 2-5/8", and the angle at which it slopes back is 8°. Instructions for cutting the mortises and tenons are given in subsequent steps.)

2. Use a jigsaw or band saw to cut out the plywood patterns; use a utility knife if the patterns are on poster board.

3. Cut two 33" rear upright blanks from one of the 1-7/8" x 5-1/2" x 6' pieces of stock.

4. Size the other two 1-7/8" x 5-1/2" x 6' pieces by ripping four 2-5/8" boards from them.

5. Cut a 46-1/4" seat back rail and a 22" arm blank from each of two 2-5/8" boards.

6. From each of the other two 2-5/8" boards, cut a 26-1/4" front upright, a 17" stretcher, and a 17" seat rail blank.

7. Cut a 46-1/4" front rail from the 4' piece of 3-1/4" stock.

8. Cut five 48" seat slats from the 1" x 2-1/2" stock.

9. Cut the 7/8" x 3" stock into seven 14" back slats.

10. Cut 1/2" x 1" x 2" tenons on the back slats' ends.

11. Transfer the arm pattern to the two 22" arm blanks.

12. Cut a 1/2" x 1" x 2" tenon and a 1/2" x 1" x 2" mortise on each arm blank, using the Arm Detail as a placement guide.

13. Then use a jigsaw or band saw to cut the curved lines of the arm.

14. Transfer the rear upright pattern to the 33" blanks, and cut the two uprights out.

15. Transfer the seat rail pattern to the two 17" seat rail blanks.

16. Cut two 1/2" x 1" x 2" tenons on each rail, and

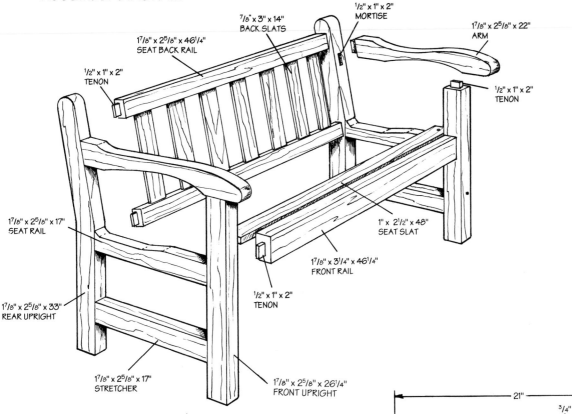

1/2" x 1" x 2"
MORTISE

7/8" x 3" x 14"
BACK SLATS

1 7/8" x 2 5/8" x 46 1/4"
SEAT BACK RAIL

1 7/8" x 2 5/8" x 22"
ARM

1/2" x 1" x 2"
TENON

1/2" x 1" x 2"
TENON

1 7/8" x 2 5/8" x 17"
SEAT RAIL

1" x 2 1/2" x 48"
SEAT SLAT

1 7/8" x 3 1/4" x 46 1/4"
FRONT RAIL

1/2" x 1" x 2"
TENON

1 7/8" x 2 5/8" x 33"
REAR UPRIGHT

1 7/8" x 2 5/8" x 17"
STRETCHER

1 7/8" x 2 5/8" x 26 1/4"
FRONT UPRIGHT

then cut around the pattern lines.

17. Cut similar tenons on the two 17" stretchers.

18. Locate the three 46-1/4" rails, and cut a 1/2" x 1" x 2" tenon on each end of all three.

19. Next, cut a 1/2" x 1" x 2" tenon on the top of each 26-1/4" front upright.

20. On the inner face of each front upright, lay out and cut a 1/2" x 1" x 2" mortise, centered 15-3/4" from the bottom.

21. On the adjacent, inner edge of each front upright, lay out and cut two 1/2" x 1" x 2" mortises, centered 15-3/8" and 5-5/8" up from the bottom.

22. Lay out and cut similar mortises at the same locations on each of the rear uprights.

23. Cut an additional mortise along the same edge of each rear upright, centered 26-1/2" up from the bottom, but cut this mortise at an 8° angle to compensate for the slope in the seat back.

24. On the inner faces of each rear upright, lay out and cut two 1/2" x 1" x 2" mortises, one centered 2-3/4" from the top and the other 17-3/8" from the top.

25. Complete the rear uprights by cutting a 1-5/16" radius half-circle on the top of each.

26. Locate the two 2-5/8" x 46-1/4" seat back rails, and clamp them together face-to-face.

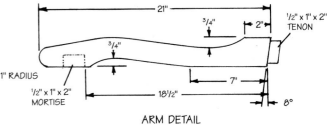

21"

3/4"

2"

1/2" x 1" x 2"
TENON

3/4"

1" RADIUS

1/2" x 1" x 2"
MORTISE

18 1/2"

7"

8°

ARM DETAIL

27. At the center of each rail, lay out a 1/2" x 1" x 2" mortise.

28. Then lay out three more mortises to each side, on 6" centers.

29. Remove the clamps, and cut the fourteen mortises.

30. Dry fit all components, and make adjustments as necessary.

31. Use epoxy resin to assemble the two side frames.

32. While the frames are drying, glue the back rest assembly, making sure that the components are square.

33. Join the two frame halves with the front rail and back rest assembly, using epoxy at the joints.

34. Glue and screw each of the five seat slats across the side rails, maintaining an equal spacing of about 3/8".

35. Sand the finished bench and apply two coats of polyurethane.

ENGLISH GARDEN BENCH

The stately English Garden Bench is the most formal of all the projects in this book, but you don't need a ten-acre garden (or ten gardeners) to enjoy it. A shaded spot between two trees, a flower-ringed patch of green lawn—almost any outdoor space that you like—can serve to highlight this magnificent piece. Don't let the bench's curved back deter you from choosing it as a project either. The graceful arc is remarkably easy to create.

ENGLISH GARDEN BENCH

SUGGESTED TOOLS

Circular saw
Combination square
Compass
Hammer
Chisel
Level
3/8" electric drill
Jigsaw
Rasp
Router (optional)
Band saw (optional)
Table saw with dado blade (optional)

MATERIALS LIST

(1) 1/2" x 7" x 62" plywood Curved bench-back pattern
(1) 1" x 7" x 62" Curved bench back
(1) 1/4" x 5-1/4" x 36" plywood Rear leg pattern
(1) 1-3/4" x 5-1/4" x 6' Rear legs
(2) 1-3/4" x 2-1/2" x 9' Front legs and rails
(1) 1-3/4" x 3-1/2" x 4' Arms
(1) 1-3/4" x 1-3/4" x 5' Stretchers
(6) 1" x 2-1/2" x 6' Seat back and bench slats
(1) 1/2" x 2-1/2" x 16' Back slats

HARDWARE & SUPPLIES

6' of pull-chain or nylon cord
Quick-drying epoxy resin
Sandpaper

Recommended Material and Finish:
red oak and polyurethane

CURVED BACK
(see Curved Back Layout)

1. The bench back will be cut from the 1" x 7" x 62" blank, but before cutting it, you'll need to establish the back's curve. To do this, stand a piece of 1/2" plywood the same size as the construction stock (7" x 62") on edge, and level it from end to end. You can do this by inserting shims under it, and checking it with the bubble gauge in your combination square.

2. Then measure and mark a point 3-3/4" down from the top edge on each end. Place a small nail at each location, and attach a length of pull-chain or heavy nylon cord to the nails, allowing the chain or cord to sag the full width of the board. The curve formed is called a catenary curve.

3. Next, trace a line around the outer edge of this curve, being careful not to disturb the chain.

4. Use a jigsaw to cut along the marked line.

5. Set your compass to a radius of 3-1/2", and use it as a scribe to form the inner (upper) curve. Do this by holding the compass at a right angle to the outer curve, with one end on that curve and the other 3-1/2" away. Sweep the compass from one end of the curve to the other end, marking an upper curve as you do.

6. Cut along the inner curve to form a continuous 1" x 3-1/2" x 62" arch.

7. Mark the left and right sides of the plywood pattern for future reference, and then set the pattern aside.

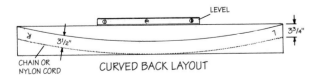

CURVED BACK LAYOUT

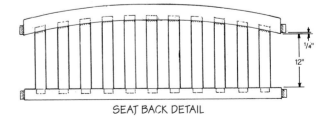

SEAT BACK DETAIL

REAR LEG
(see Assembly Diagram and Rear Leg Detail)

8. Next, you'll need to lay out the rear leg pattern on a piece of 1/4" x 5-1/4" x 36" plywood. Place the plywood in front of you, on a level surface, so that its long sides run up and down. Measure and draw a straight, vertical line (starting at the bottom of the plywood), 17-1/2" long and 2-1/2" from the left side of the blank.

9. From the 17-1/2" point, angle the line back approximately 8°, and continue it until it intersects with the upper right-hand corner of the plywood blank.

10. Return to the point at which the line changed course (at 17-1/2"). From the edge of the plywood opposite to that point, draw a straight line parallel to the angled line and 2-1/2" away from it. Cut the leg pattern out. You may want to include a rounded corner on each leg's upper end.

11. Cut the 1-3/4" x 5-1/4" x 6' stock in half, and transfer the rear leg pattern to each half.

12. With a jigsaw, cut out the two rear leg blanks.

13. Lay out and cut the six mortises in each rear leg. Be sure to refer to the illustration for correct mortise placement.

FRONT LEGS
(see Assembly Diagram and Front Leg Detail)

14. Cut a 1-3/4" x 2-1/2" x 25-1/2" front leg blank from each of the two 9' pieces of stock.

15. Lay out and cut the three mortises and one tenon on each leg. Refer to the illustrations for correct placement.

FRONT, BACK, AND SIDE RAILS
(see Assembly Diagram)

16. From each of the two remaining pieces of 1-3/4" x 2-1/2" stock, cut a 62" and 17" rail.

17. Cut a 1/2" x 1" x 2" tenon on both ends of each of these four pieces.

18. Cut a 1/2" x 1" x 1-1/4" mortise in the center of each 62" rail.

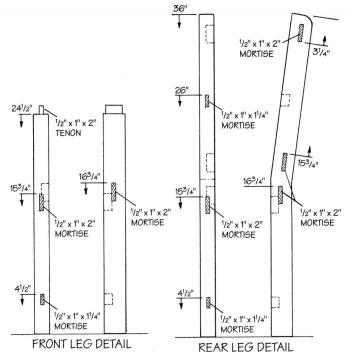

FRONT LEG DETAIL   REAR LEG DETAIL

ARMS
(see Arm Detail)

19. Cut two 22-1/2" arm blanks from the 4' section of 1-3/4" x 3-1/2" stock.

20. With a jigsaw, taper both edges of each arm from the full 3-1/2" width to 1-3/4". Then round off the wide ends with either a router and 3/4" rounding-over bit or with a rasp. If you'd rather, you can round the wide end of the arm by cutting a 1-3/4" radius half-circle instead; the arm variations shown with the Chippendale Bench are also possible.

21. Finish each arm by cutting a 1/2" x 1" x 1-1/4" tenon on the narrow end, and a 1/2" x 1" x 2" mortise, 3-1/4" back from the front edge. Note in the Arm Detail that the narrow end of the arm is tapered at an 8° angle from the tenon.

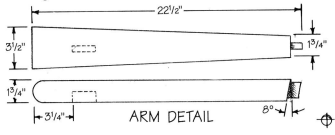

ARM DETAIL

STRETCHERS
(see Assembly Diagram)

22. To form the stretchers, cut two 17" sections and one 17-3/4" section from the 1-3/4" x 1-3/4" stock.

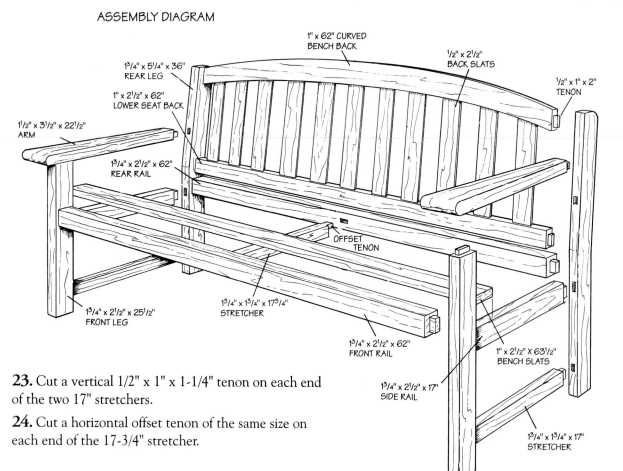

1" x 62" CURVED
BENCH BACK

1³/4" x 5¹/4" x 36"
REAR LEG

1" x 2¹/2" x 62"
LOWER SEAT BACK

¹/2" x 2¹/2"
BACK SLATS

¹/2" x 1" x 2"
TENON

1¹/2" x 3¹/2" x 22¹/2"
ARM

1³/4" x 2¹/2" x 62"
REAR RAIL

OFFSET
TENON

1³/4" x 2¹/2" x 25¹/2"
FRONT LEG

1³/4" x 1³/4" x 17³/4"
STRETCHER

1³/4" x 2¹/2" x 62"
FRONT RAIL

1" x 2¹/2" X 63¹/2"
BENCH SLATS

1³/4" x 2¹/2" x 17"
SIDE RAIL

1³/4" x 1³/4" x 17"
STRETCHER

23. Cut a vertical 1/2" x 1" x 1-1/4" tenon on each end of the two 17" stretchers.

24. Cut a horizontal offset tenon of the same size on each end of the 17-3/4" stretcher.

SEAT BACK
(see Seat Back Detail)

25. From one of the 1" x 2-1/2" pieces of stock, cut a 62" lower seat back.

26. Cut a 1/2" x 1" x 2" tenon on each of its ends.

27. Lay the curved back pattern on top of the 1" x 7" x 62" stock. Position the pattern so that the ends of the inner curve intersect with the lower outside corners of the board.

28. Transfer the pattern to the stock with a pencil.

29. With a jigsaw, cut around the inner (or lower) curve.

30. At each end of the board, cut a 1/2" x 1" x 2" tenon, leaving a 1/4" shoulder at the bottom. Do not cut the outer curve yet.

31. Position and clamp the upper (curved) and lower backs firmly so that they are square and separated by a distance of 12" at each end.

32. Cut eleven 17" back slats from the 1/2" x 2-1/2" x 16' stock.

33. Space these slats about 2-3/4" apart beneath the upper and lower backs.

34. With a pencil, mark the position of each back slat on the two back pieces, and mark the exposed length of each slat on the slat itself. Number each slat for future ease of assembly.

35. Allow for a 1/4" x 1" x 2" tenon at the bottom of each slat and an additional 1-1/4" material at the top of each slat.

36. Cut the renons on each slat's bottom end, and round the corners of the excess material at the top.

37. Use a drill to begin corresponding mortises in the upper and lower backs. Finish these mortises with a hammer and chisel.

38. Dry fit and adjust all slats.

39. Cut the top curve of the bench back piece with a jigsaw.

40. Sand all the components.

41. Dry fit the entire bench (minus bench slats), and make adjustments as necessary.

42. Apply quick-drying epoxy resin to all joints, and then assemble.

SEAT SLATS
(see Assembly Diagram)

43. Cut and then sand five 63-1/2" bench slats from the remaining 1" x 2-1/2" x 6' pieces.

44. When the bench is dry, space the slats equally across the side rails, and epoxy them in place.

45. Finish the assembled bench by applying two coats of polyurethane.

LUMBER SIZING, DIMENSIONS, AND GRADES

SIZING AND DIMENSIONS

Unless you're fortunate enough to have access to custom-ordered project stock, the wood you're likely to purchase will meet the standards of the various manufacturing associations which govern the wood products industry.

A piece of softwood lumber less than 1" thick and between 2" and 6" wide is called a strip. Wood less than 2" thick and up to 16" wide falls into the board category. Dimension lumber measures from 2" to 4-1/2" thick and up to 16" wide, and timbers must have at least a 5" dimension on any side surface. Standard lengths range from 6' or 8' to 16', in 2-foot increments.

All lumber is sized and priced by its rough, mill-sawn dimensions, but when the raw stock is planed, as it needs to be for the market, its overall size can be reduced by 25% or more. For this reason, lumber sizes are given as either nominal or actual sizes. The term nominal refers to the original sawn dimensions. After planing, the piece is sold at its actual dimensions. The actual measurements of a nominal 2 x 4, for instance, are only 1-1/2" x 3-1/2".

Hardwoods are sized somewhat differently. Boards come in random widths up to 6", though for certain grades minimum widths are specified. Standard lengths run from 4' to 16'. Thickness is generally measured in 1/4" gradations, from 1" to 4", and is expressed as a fraction. A 5/4 board measures 1-1/4" before it's planed.

Hardwood can be sold as rough (when it's unplaned) or surfaced (when it's been planed on one or more sides). A board labelled S2S indicates that it's been surfaced on two sides. Softwood lumber, as well, can be surfaced; this is usually done with board products such as shelving.

Wood is sold in volume by the board foot, a long-established standard by which each unit is equivalent to a rough board measuring 1" thick by 12" wide by 12" long, or 144 cubic inches. Any stock less than an inch thick is counted as a full inch, and anything over an inch in thickness is figured to the next largest 1/4". In practice, then, a 6'-long 1 x 6 contains 3 board feet—and so does a piece measuring 1-3/8" x 2" x 12'. To calculate board feet, multiply thickness by width in inches; then multiply the result by length in feet and divide by 12. Dimensional lumber retailed for construction is often sold by the piece to make consumer billing easier, but the prices are still based on board-foot calculations.

Plywood—a manufactured product made of thin layers or veneers glued so that adjacent grains run at a perpendicular to one another—comes in a standard 4' x 8' panel. Panels are available in 3/16" thicknesses and in sizes that run from 1/4" to 3/4", in 1/8" increments. A 1" thickness is manufactured but would probably have to be special-ordered.

GRADES

Technically speaking, lumber is wood cut from trees, which is then sawed and sold by standard dimensions. When a log is sawed, it yields lumber which varies in quality, however. To assure that buyers get a product that suits their needs, the lumber is graded into categories that reflect a standard quality range.

The grade is based on the size of the wood and on the number and significance of defects (knots, pitch pockets, etc.) that compromise the strength, utility, or durability of the finished product. Hardwoods and softwoods are each graded further by use, taking species, appearance, and structural integrity into account.

The softwood grades of interest to the consumer are those established for construction. (A separate industrial grading system applies to other than consumer woods.) Construction grades are broken down into three categories: stress-graded, non-stress graded, and appearance.

Stress-graded lumber includes framing pieces, timbers, decking, and structural stair components. This is an American-Canadian standard which meets an established set of criteria.

The grade names—Construction, Standard, and Utility (for light framing), and Stud (for pieces 10' and shorter)—are assigned, as indicated, according to use or classification.

Non-stress graded lumber is yard stock used for general building purposes and includes boards, planks, and lath. The boards are called commons and fall into five different grades depending on species. No. 1 boards have tight knots and minor blemishes and are used for finish work; No. 2 have larger knots and noticeable blemishes and are suitable for flooring and panelling; No. 3 contain knotholes and visible flaws and are fine for sheathing and fencing; Nos. 4 and 5 are boards of low quality; they have limited strength. You should be aware that some manufacturing associations use names rather than numbers to assign grades: Select, Merchantable, and Construction (or Colonial, Sterling, and Standard) correspond roughly—but not literally—to the number grades.

Appearance lumber is not stress-graded, but is visually appealing. It's generally used for finish work and is graded into two categories—Finish and Select. Select grades are described by letters, numbers, and names. Hence, B & Btr (1 and 2 Clear) is a product of higher quality than C Select, which contains limited defects. D Select grade has minor surface imperfections. Named species, such as Idaho white pine, are categorized by the labels Supreme, Choice, and Quality.

Hardwood lumber is graded into three categories, but in the United States, only the "factory" grades established by the National Hardwood Lumber Association apply to consumer woods. They're based on the proportion of a piece that can be sawn into a number of smaller cuttings, which are sorted further into three grades.

"Firsts and seconds" (FAS) is a combination of the two best grades; the boards must be at least 6" wide and 8' long. Selects are FAS-quality boards at least 4" wide and 6' in length. No 1. common—often called shorts—is the lowest grade of project hardwood, limited to a minimum 3" width and 4' length.

Plywood panels can be constructed of softwood (Douglas fir, western hemlock, and pine) or hardwood (birch, oak, cherry, and walnut.) In the United States, plywood grades are established by the quality of the face and back veneers. The inspection stamps on the back of each panel show the grade of both sides, the wood species group number (lower numbers indicate stiffer panels), application for interior or exterior use, and the mill and testing marks.

Softwood panels are graded by letter: N—suitable for a natural finish and free of open defects; A—smooth and paintable, limited to 18 neatly-made repairs; B—solid surfaced, with circular repair plugs and tight knots; C—knotholes up to 1" and tight knots to 1-1/2", with limited splits allowed.

Hardwood panels use number grades: 1—premium, book-matched grain with only minor defects; 1—good, but unmatched grain and minor defects; 2—sound, suitable for painting, with appearance defects and smooth patches.

METRIC EQUIVALENCY CHART

Inches	MM	CM
1/8	3	.3
1/4	6	.6
3/8	10	1.0
1/2	13	1.3
5/8	16	1.6
3/4	19	1.9
7/8	22	2.2
1	25	2.5
1-1/4	32	3.2
1-1/2	38	3.8
1-3/4	44	4.4
2	51	5.1
2-1/2	64	6.4
3	76	7.6
3-1/2	89	8.9
4	102	10.2
4-1/2	114	11.4
5	127	12.7
6	152	15.2
7	178	17.8
8	203	20.3
9	229	22.9
10	254	25.4
11	279	27.9
12	305	30.5
13	330	33.0
14	356	35.6
15	381	38.1
16	406	40.6
17	432	43.2
18	457	45.7
19	483	48.3
20	508	50.8
21	533	53.3
22	559	55.9
23	584	58.4
24	610	61.0
25	635	63.5
26	660	66.0
27	686	68.6
28	711	71.1
29	737	73.7
30	762	76.2
31	787	78.7
32	813	81.3
33	838	83.8
34	864	86.4
35	889	88.9
36	914	91.4
37	940	94.0
38	965	96.5
39	991	99.1
40	1,016	101.6
41	1,041	104.1
42	1,067	106.7
43	1,092	109.2
44	1,118	111.8
45	1,143	114.3
46	1,168	116.8
47	1,194	119.4
48	1,219	121.9
49	1,245	124.5
50	1,270	127.0

ACKNOWLEDGEMENTS

ADDITIONAL PHOTOGRAPHS

Special thanks to Mr. HENRY LANZ of the Garrett Wade Company, who very generously provided the photographs on pages 10, 14, 17, 20, 21, 24, and 29. The fine tools shown are available through Garrett Wade, 161 Avenue of the Americas, New York, NY 10013. The Garrett Wade Tool Catalog is distributed by Sterling Publishing Company, Inc., 387 Park Avenue South, New York, NY 10016.

..and to LYNN LECHOWICZ, Marketing Communications Supervisor at Black & Decker (U.S.), Inc., for having provided the black-and-white photographs on pages 18, 19, and 30.

SOFTWOOD SIZES

Nominal	Actual
1 x 2	3/4" x 1-1/2"
1 x 3	3/4" x 2-1/2"
1 x 4	3/4" x 3-1/2"
1 x 5	3/4" x 4-1/2"
1 x 6	3/4" x 5-1/2"
1 x 8	3/4" x 7-1/4"
1 x 10	3/4" x 9-1/4"
1 x 12	3/4" x 11-1/4"
2 x 2	1-1/2" x 1-1/2"
2 x 4	1-1/2" x 3-1/2"
2 x 6	1-1/2" x 5-1/2"
2 x 8	1-1/2" x 7-1/4"
2 x 10	1-1/2" x 9-1/4"
2 x 12	1-1/2" x 11-1/4"
4 x 4	3-1/2" x 3-1/2"
4 x 6	3-1/2" x 5-1/2"
6 x 6	5-1/2" x 5-1/2"
8 x 8	7-1/2" x 7-1/2"

LOCATION PHOTOGRAPHY

For their assistance with location photography, thanks to SUE ALEXANDER, Vice-President of the Great Outdoors Garden Shop & Landscape Company, EDWARD A. GIBSON, JR., Secretary\Treasurer of B.B. Barns, Inc., (both in Asheville, NC), and ALLEN BUSH of Holbrook Farms (Fletcher, NC).

Many thanks to the following garden owners, all residents of the Asheville, NC area:

JAN AND SIMON BRAUN

ALLEN BUSH

JOHN CRAM

JASMINE AND PETER GENTLING

PETER LOEWER

THE UNIVERITY OF NORTH CAROLINA AT ASHEVILLE, BOTANICAL GARDENS

CATHY AND PETER WALLENBORN

DIANE AND DICK WEAVER

Also thanks to...

DON OSBY (Horse Shoe, NC), owner of Page One Publications, for his illustrations and for his help with the project instructions.

RICHARD FREUDENBERGER (Hendersonville, NC), Executive Editor of *Back Home* magazine, for his invaluable help in writing Chapter Two.

INDEX